ABSTRACT
PAINTING AND SCULPTURE
IN AMERICA

ABSTRACT

PAINTING AND SCULPTURE

IN AMERICA

by Andrew Carnduff Ritchie

The Museum of Modern Art   New York

CONTENTS

ACKNOWLEDGMENTS

On behalf of the President and Trustees of the Museum of Modern Art the director of the exhibition wishes to thank the collectors, museums and dealers whose generosity in lending has made the exhibition possible. Particular thanks are due to Alfred H. Barr, Jr., to whose book, *Cubism and Abstract Art*, all who touch the subject of abstraction must always be indebted; to Miss Margaret Miller for her advice and assistance throughout; to Miss Alice Bacon for research assistance; to Miss Alice Wilson for her work in the preparation of the catalogue; to Erik Nitsche for the design of the cover; to Miss Dorothy Miller and Holger Cahill for advice and help in locating some of the earlier, now historical, paintings in the exhibition; to Lloyd Goodrich, Mrs. Wolfgang S. Schwabacher and Julien Levy for assistance in the selection of works by Gorky; to Hudson Walker for advice on the abstract paintings of Hartley; to George Heard Hamilton, John Marshall Phillips and Lamont Moore for their help in selecting works from the *Société Anonyme* Collection at Yale University; and to Walter Pach, Stanton Macdonald-Wright, Man Ray and William Zorach for information on the early years of abstract art in this country.

ANDREW CARNDUFF RITCHIE
Director of the Exhibition

PREFACE

In 1936 the Museum of Modern Art presented an exhibition entitled *Cubism and Abstract Art*. In the preface to the catalogue, Alfred H. Barr, Jr. states that the exhibition is restricted to European examples of Cubism and abstraction, since a year previously the Whitney Museum had shown a large collection of abstract art in America.

Now, fifteen years later, with the production of abstract painting and sculpture steadily increasing in this country it has seemed appropriate to review the movement in both a historical and contemporary sense. This exhibition covers a period of approximately thirty-seven years, from about the time of the famous Armory Show of 1913 to the present. The origins of 20th century abstract art are in Europe, but certain American artists reacted almost immediately to the first stirrings of the movement; consequently the period covered in this exhibition coincides fairly well with the history of abstract art abroad.

The selection of paintings and sculpture here presented has been made by the author. It does not pretend to be representative of all American artists who have expressed themselves, or are expressing themselves, in abstract terms. The length of time covered by the exhibition and limitations of space made such an all-inclusive show impossible. Rather, this is a personal choice which seeks to display, at as high a level of quality as possible, enough distinctive examples of abstract painting and sculpture produced by Americans, or foreigners long resident in America, to give the observer and reader a sufficient appreciation of the variety and extent of this form of art in this country. Furthermore, the emphasis in the selection has been placed upon the more extreme directions of the abstract movement. The reader or observer may then better judge its validity.

Space limitations have, regrettably, made impossible any consideration of abstract prints and photographs.

A. C. R.

. . . Painting is nothing but an image of incorporeal things, despite the fact that it exhibits bodies, for it represents only the arrangements, proportions, and forms of things, and is more intent on the idea of beauty than on any other.

> Nicolas Poussin
> *From Observations on Painting*, quoted by
> Goldwater and Treves, *Artists on Art*, p. 156

In *A New Method of Assisting the Invention in Drawing Original Compositions of Landscape* he [Alexander Cozens, c. 1715-1786] describes how he accidentally hit on the device of working up a casual blot of ink or sepia into the composition its shapes suggested. And he tells of his joy in discovering that Leonardo had been before him, with his advice to study the rough texture of an old wall for suggestions of landscape form; he would have rejoiced still more if he had known that a Chinese painter had been before Leonardo with similar advice.

> Lawrence Binyon
> *English Water-Colours*, p. 42

I . . . think I understand *why* so many great colorists, especially Tintoret and Paul Veronese, gave so little heed to the ostensible *stories* of their compositions. In some of them . . . there is not the slightest clue given by which the spectator can guess at the subject. They addressed themselves, not to the senses merely . . . but rather through them to that region (if I may so speak) of the imagination which is supposed to be under the exclusive dominion of music. . . .

> Washington Allston
> Quoted by James Thrall Soby,
> *Romantic Painting in America*, p. 12

10

WHAT IS ABSTRACT ART?

The term "abstract" has a negative connotation. In common language it means to remove, to take away. In this sense all art is abstract to some degree. However accurately in detail a painter may attempt to describe a portion of nature, inevitably some minute particle of reality will escape his observation; or he may consciously, or unconsciously, "abstract" it from his representation in the interests of clarification, that is to say, art. Flemish and German realist painters of the 15th and 16th centuries were artists of this kind. Renaissance Italians practiced another type of abstraction, a synthesis of abstracted forms in order to present an ideal face or landscape which was thought to be superior to any particular face or landscape in nature. This synthetic abstraction was an inheritance, in part, from the Greeks and since the Renaissance has been practiced by all artists trained in the so-called academic tradition. Sir Joshua Reynolds in the tenth of his *Discourses* went so far as to call this method the "science of abstract form."

In the history of ornament and in the arts of primitive and prehistoric peoples all kinds of abstract and near abstract designs are common. The fret motif of the Greeks and the interlace ornaments of the Scandinavian and Celtic tribes, the geometric abstraction of form in African, Oceanic and early Chinese sculpture and the Arabic use of calligraphy for decoration—all are familiar examples of one or another kind of abstract art in the past.

While abstract art is not a new phenomenon, it must be emphasized that it has never until the 20th century played a particularly dominant role in the history of Western art. One distinguishing characteristic of the realist and academic painter in this Western tradition is that both address themselves to "nature," the one particularizing, the other generalizing his observations as much as he sees fit. Twentieth-century abstract art, on the contrary, in its "purest" states, at least, removes itself completely from all references to traditional aspects of nature or conventional ideas of subject matter. At one extreme, this "pure" abstraction becomes an art of precisely coordinated geometrical shapes and spectrum colors. This might be called the classical or intellectual pole. The other extreme resolves itself into a pictorial

11

organism made up of interrelated biomorphic forms or calligraphic interlacings. Colors are not necessarily of spectrum purity and are used for emotional effect. This might be called the romantic or expressionist pole. Between these extremes there are degrees of abstraction which have a greater or lesser relation to the representation of natural forms. As a general rule, the human or animal figure plays an exceedingly small role in any kind of 20th century abstract art. Where reference exists to objects, in the between-extremes of abstraction, it is more often to inanimate forms, mechanical or architectural.

Stated in another way, one may say that both extremes of abstract artists in our time have experimented on a partly instinctive, partly intellectual plane with space, form and color, all more or less removed from any associations outside the picture frame. Taking the canvas as a two-dimensional area, abstract artists have sought to make the space defined by the canvas an end in itself. Likewise, the forms and colors within this picture space are intended to present a life of their own, undiluted by any reference to exterior prototypes. This is a severe program of creation indeed, and some attempt must be made here to explain how and why many contemporary European and American artists have been led to such a position.

WHY ABSTRACT ART?

The invention of the camera and the consequent boredom of artists with "nature," the influence of the machine, new scientific discoveries, the parallel of music—all have been used by way of argument or explanation for the impulse toward abstraction. Each of these explanations has some justification, but all of them tend to beg as many questions as they answer. Before proceeding to what I think are the fundamental motivations for abstract art we may, however, look briefly at the above explanations one by one.

The Invention of the Camera and the Taste for Literal Realism

The invention of still and moving picture cameras has played an important part in making obsolete a large element of the artist's skill—the mere representation of natural appearances. If we take the abandonment of naturalistic representation as a *sine qua non* of abstract art, it is not hard to understand why certain artists, after the perfection of the camera, felt logically driven to find another kind of outlet for their creative talents.

The mere representation of natural appearances was not, however, a dominant factor in Western art until the 19th century. The fact that for many reasons it became a necessary artistic pursuit to appeal to the taste of literal-minded patrons is, in fact, one of the reasons for the invention of the camera. Long before the camera, there were in existence mechanical optical aides to assist the artist who wished to document nature accurately. When the demand for such documentation became sufficiently widespread, as it did in the 19th century, the invention of the camera, one can say, became inevitable. It is not enough to say, then, that certain artists

Surface of the moon. *Photograph courtesy Lick Observatory*   Airview of ocean. *Official U.S. Navy photograph*

lost interest in competing with the camera. Fundamentally, they lost interest in and resisted the taste for the literal representation of nature which had been partly responsible for the introduction of the camera. This difference in taste between the creative artist and the public became more pronounced as the 19th century advanced, until finally a serious divorce between them could not be denied.

The Parallel of Music

Some abstract artists have been motivated by an urge towards a universal language of color and rhythm that would take the place of subject matter whose reference was limited to the local or national scene. They saw in music—perhaps the most universal emotional language of the 19th century—which in large part lacked any reference to natural sounds or literary story, a justification for abstract painting. However fallacious this parallel is (the one art deals in intervals of time, the other in intervals of space, and auditory and visual rhythms affect our nervous systems quite differently), it was used by artists, like the Russian Wassily Kandinsky, to justify what they considered to be the emotional, even mystical, appeal of their pictures to a mass audience. This is, by the way, a significant reversal of the position of those artists who painted for the picture's sake and the devil take the unsympathetic public.

New Scientific Discoveries

In speaking above of abstract art in relation to "nature," it is nature in the traditional, conventional, practically static sense that is referred to. The concept of nature has, of course, been greatly expanded in our time to include a new world of

13

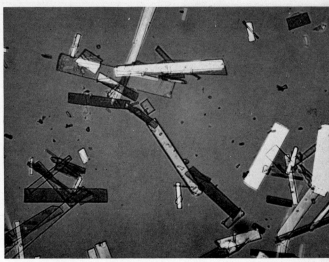

Stars. *Photograph courtesy Yerkes Observatory*   Digitoxin crystals. *Photograph Keturah Blakely*

phenomena. More powerful microscopes have enormously increased our knowledge of the structure of matter and living organisms. Larger telescopes have visually extended our exploration of astronomical space. The stroboscopic camera has given us an exact picture of objects moving at high speed. The airplane permits us to view any part of the earth or sea at heights and speeds undreamed of before. In short, chemical, physical and mathematical discoveries have given us a more extensive view of the universe. Our concepts of time and space have been altered, and their relative interaction has forced us to abandon fixed measures of both, at least on the scientific level of our thinking.

It would be a dangerous assumption to contend that abstract art is merely a product of or a reaction to these new scientific discoveries. Nevertheless, there are some indications that many abstract artists reflect in their work an awareness, conscious or unconscious, of the new world of nature that is every day being revealed to us.

The Influence of the Machine

While science has provided us with a greatly enriched concept of nature, it has also produced for our technological age an army of machines. Paradoxically, these machines have often tended to divert our attention from nature itself, and because of their seemingly dominant place in our civilization, certain artists, like Léger, have accepted the machine's cylindrical and cubic forms as a basis for their paintings. The result is one kind of geometric abstraction which, however "impure" it may be and however bound it is to the subject matter of machines themselves, has played a significant role in the abstract movement.

14

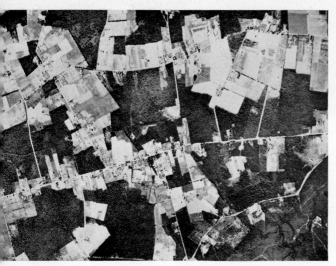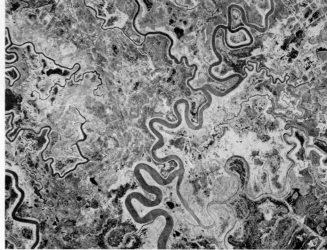

Two airviews. *Photographs courtesy Sibyl Moholy-Nagy*

ABSTRACTION AND PROTEST

A common factor running through all the above reasons for, or motivations towards, abstract art is *protest*. Protest against the established order of traditional perspective, naturalistic space and color, conventional subject matter. All modern, advance-guard art movements have been protests, of course, but abstract art is the most protestant of all. Actually these movements of art protest are paralleled by a new age of democratic protest that has been under way since the 18th century. And as with the religious Reformation, the Democratic reformation has called up many counter movements to arrest or neutralize its progress. There is, in short, a broad pattern to all protestant movements, be they religious, social, economic or artistic: a period of wrestling with the established order; leading to a more or less violent break with that order by puritanical and evangelical revolutionaries; leading in turn to the formation of splinter revolutionary parties; and finally to counter-revolutionary groups. Looked at from this standpoint, abstract artists are the leading artistic revolutionaries of our day and like their fellows in other revolutionary movements they are attracted to intellectual or emotional extremes. Just as we have strictly rational Calvinists and emotional evangelicals in religion, and in politics evolutionary socialists and violent, revolutionary communists, or hierarchically minded Federalists and Populists appealing to the masses, so we have abstract artists who believe in a strict geometrical theology and those who preach a visceral gospel, appealing to the instinctive or unconscious reflexes.

While abstract art is an art of protest it is not, like other rebel movements, a mere protest against an immediately preceding style. It is a culmination of many revolu-

15

tions dating back to the 17th century. And it contains within itself the residue of many of the points of protest in these past revolutions.

A Revolutionary Change in the State of Patronage

The greatest break in the tradition of Western art, a tradition going back to Greece and over two thousand years old, came in the 18th century about the time of the French Revolution. This break was closely connected with a fundamental change in the state of patronage, which grew out of the great social and economic changes produced in part by Protestantism, with all its emphasis on individual faith, and Democracy, with all its emphasis on individual freedom.

Before the French Revolution there were important indications of this revolution in patronage in both 17th century Holland and 18th century England, two Protestant countries which largely as a concomitant of their Protestantism fought to destroy the combined tyrannies of Church and King. Now, as it happened, before these Protestant revolutions, the artist had largely been dependent on the Church, the King and the nobility for his livelihood. (There are, it is true, significant exceptions to this generalization: particularly in the Low Countries and Germany, where the governing authority was often of a foreign or absentee kind.) He was their servant and they were his patrons and the art he produced was calculated to appeal to their taste. The American Revolution and finally the French put an emphatic end to this association. The Church and the aristocracy continued, of course, and still continue, to provide some art patronage, but it has become an extremely unimportant factor so far as the great majority of artists is concerned. (There are minute signs of a revival of Church patronage in England and France at the moment, but they are so local and unorganized they are of no account in the larger scheme of things.)

As the Church and the nobility receded in importance as patrons, the almost impersonal middle-class buyer took their place. The important thing about this burgher patron in Holland and his business fellow in England was that they had, unlike their older patrons, no inherited prejudices of taste. Until they felt strong enough to assert themselves, culturally speaking, they did, of course, ape their "betters" for a time. In general, after the French Revolution and the extraordinary growth of the Industrial Revolution in the 19th century, the business man dominated the whole world of patronage.

This business man and the society of which he became the ruling head had little knowledge of the established theories of artistic creation, the accumulated critical thought dating back to the Renaissance. This criticism, summed up to a great extent in Sir Joshua Reynolds' *Discourses*, held to a kind of hierarchy of subject matter and style. It held in highest esteem all painting and sculpture which was related to classical concepts of poetry. Agreeing with Aristotle, it accepted poetry, particularly epic poetry, as the greatest achievement of the human mind and emotions. Painting and sculpture which in subject matter emulated great poetry were therefore considered of the highest order. And as in this classical scheme the language of great poetry had to be of an ideal, as it was called, or uncommon kind and not of a literal or common persuasion, so the greatest painting and sculpture, following such precepts, had in style to present the scenes and personages of poetic or biblical history and mythology in an ideal manner. The scene itself could be no ordinary, particularized landscape or interior; the characters must not be common or individual in feature or costume. The lower levels in this aesthetic hierarchy, and they were far below so-called "history" painting, were portraiture (to idealize in the "grand" manner and still retain a "good likeness" was a difficult compromise at best), landscape (a similar compromise was demanded between literal documentation and an ideal improvement of nature) and, lowest of all, still life.

Now consider your business man or industrialist patron, or for that matter the people at large, in the 19th century. Lacking the necessary leisure they were not "educated" in the traditional, aristocratic sense. Their knowledge of poetry and history was sketchy at best and of artistic theories they knew practically nothing. They knew the Bible in great detail (far better than we know it today) but only sentimental or story-telling religious pictures were in wide demand. In the latter connection, Protestants of every description have been either mildly or violently opposed to representations of the Divinity, considering them idolatrous. In Catholic countries, on the other hand, particularly France, the powerful anti-clerical feeling in all classes of society, which was a factor in and a residue from the French Revolution, acted as a deterrent on the production of any profound or serious religious art for non-church use, or even for the Church itself.

What of the artist in this society—a society which was democratic, industrial, relatively uneducated in any traditional sense? First of all, with his old personal contacts with particular church and aristocratic patrons declining or non-existent, he found himself in an increasingly separate relationship with his new public. Where previously the patron had often come to the artist with a specific commission or to choose a particular picture or sculpture in his workshop or studio, now the artist was faced with a greatly enlarged, but for him, impersonal, patronage and one whose artistic values or taste were in a confused, not to say chaotic state. Out of this chaos, one thing soon became clear to even the most simple-minded artist. This new patron, unschooled in classical imagery, demanded a kind of subject matter he could understand. If the picture told a story, it must be one he was familiar with or whose dramatic or emotional implications were not beyond his limited reading experience or aspirations. These demands proved to be best filled by paintings of sentimental anecdotes of a mildly humorous or "moral" nature. If the artist chose to depict a landscape, it must be one this new patron considered believable in a literal sense but which according to his simple taste was either "pretty," and by no means reminiscent of the squalor and ugliness of his industrial surroundings, or "grand" in a melodramatic, spectacular sense. In portraiture he demanded a "romantic," pretty treatment of women, again as far removed as possible from his own business or industrial associations. For himself he preferred a no-nonsense "likeness" that would do justice, nevertheless, to his own sense of self-importance. As for still life, he seems to have been best pleased with a fool-the-eye rendering of objects and quite properly accepted such pictures more as *tours de force* of the artist's skill, the magic of his brush, so to speak, rather than as significant works of art. The American, Harnett, was such a popular "magic realist" both here and in Europe. Germany, however, and particularly Munich, was the principal source for most of this kind of painting.

The style of execution this work-a-day patron preferred was closely related to his own requirements in business or industry. He accepted the technical methods, however watered down, inherited from Renaissance practice: the adherence to the traditional rules of a statically observed, vanishing point perspective; a conceptual, and not wholly optical, definition of forms by means of a minutely graduated rendering of light and shade—the light and shade of the studio, not of the out-of-doors; and the careful delineation of a form or figure—that is to say, "good" drawing. In short, most 19th century patrons and the public taste they determined were partial rebels as to subject matter but favored a conservative execution or style, however debased. They would have nothing to do with an ancient mythology, history or legend unknown to them but they were willing to accept in their place familiar, sentimental anecdotes, well-known scenes from their own national history or easily comprehensible narrative pictures, preferably with amusing or moralistic implications. In execution, however, they were willing to accept without question all the traditional paraphernalia of the art schools, however vulgarized. In the latter respect they were like all church or secular patrons of art before them: they insisted upon the right to control subject matter but within certain limits, largely induced by fashion, they left the artist free to evolve his own style of expression or execution.*

The art schools of the 19th century were either attached to those depositories of stylistic tradition, the academies, or were controlled by academicians. By dint of royal and aristocratic support the academies in Europe had made themselves since the 17th century the official arbiters in all matters connected with artistic execution and technique. They were able to exert their control by various means: by limiting the number of artist members who might belong to the academy and thus giving individual members an "official" professional reputation in the community they might not otherwise have possessed; by controlling the teaching of art students they ensured a respect for academic methods of art production and a continuation of it into the future. They continue today to exert a certain amount of influence and nowhere as powerfully—an inheritance from the Czarist academy—as in Russia.

Rebel Artists and the Gradual Dissolution of Conventional Subject Matter

What of the 19th century artist, unable to accept academic subject matter and technique and the popular patronage they had attracted? He naturally found him-

* I believe the only instances in the history of art when the patron has insisted on determining not only *what* an artist says or paints or composes but also *how* he shall say or paint or compose have occurred in our own times. The Nazis, following the example of the Soviet Union, placed these absolute controls upon artists—controls comparable to those forced upon all their other subjects—and the Soviet Union continues these controls today.

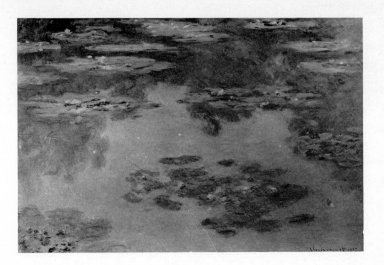

Monet: *Nymphaea: Waterscape.* 1907. Oil.
The Art Institute of Chicago

self painting for a very restricted public and often only for himself. In any case, the picture became of first importance to him, since the patron was usually an unknown entity who might not appear, as with Cézanne and van Gogh, until after the artist's death. In this studio void the artist inevitably became more and more introspective, self-conscious, if you like, a lonely explorer associating only with his own kind, if at all. Needless to say, like all rebels he was in a minority. The majority of artists gratified public taste and made a reasonable and sometimes a fancy income from their work.

The important point for us here, however, is that the rebel minority became largely separated from public patronage. This isolation, *as a condition of work*, experienced by such artists as Courbet, Manet, Monet, Pissarro, Degas, Seurat, Gauguin, van Gogh—to name a few of the greatest—was inherited on an even more intensified scale by experimental artists of this century. And, as is well known, all of them have had to suffer misunderstanding, ridicule and abuse. And many of them, as is equally well known, have answered abuse with defiance of the public. Most important, however, for an understanding of the final impulse towards abstraction is that as the experimental artist, searching for new means of expression, exploring new potentialities of his art, was driven in on himself and away from popular patronage, he paid less and less attention to subject matter as such and more and more to picture making *per se*. One of the final stages in this process is abstract art.

One of the most significant developments in this process is surely the reversal, by the first rebels, of the academic hierarchy in subject matter. While it would take volumes to study all the ramifications of this reversal, it will be sufficient for our purpose here to outline the broad features of this momentous upset. First of all, the illustrative, "literary" picture so dear to the hearts of the academicians was thrown overboard. The first signs of this rebellion are to be found in 17th century Holland

19

and 18th century England. The emphasis in the art of both on the lower levels of the academic scale of subject matter is highly significant—low-life genre, the portrait, landscape, and, with the curious exception of England, still life. In the 19th century Constable and Turner, by their concentration upon landscape, and consequently their elevation of it to a primary position in the subject scale, probably did more than any other two painters of their time to shake the foundations of the academic tradition. Courbet and, to a lesser degree, the Barbizon School, nailed the landscape banner still higher on the ramparts of academicism. The Impressionists, particularly the extremist Monet, completed the victory of landscape over all other forms of painting. More significantly still, they concentrated upon what to them was a semi-scientific, objective method of light registration, more or less "pure" colors applied in patches, fused in the eye of the observer rather than on the palette of the painter. By so concentrating, they abstracted the forms of things, that is to say their substantial attributes at least, and gave all their attention to a rendering of the instantaneous effects of light on forms. This abstract character of Impressionism cannot be emphasized too much (ill. p. 19). Impressionism has so often been wrongly called the last stage in naturalistic painting, its contrary significance as the first movement pointing forward to the "pure" abstract painting and sculpture we know today has been underestimated.

Impressionist light abstraction produced two important results for the future of abstract painting. First it undermined, unconsciously perhaps, the observer's interest in landscape as representational subject matter and thus opened the door to the abstraction of *all* representational subject matter from painting. Secondly, by

SEURAT: *Le Chahut.* 1889. Oil.
Albright Art Gallery, Buffalo

CÉZANNE: *Still Life*. 1904-06. Watercolor.
Collection Lord Ivor S. Churchill, London

concentrating narrowly upon a technique of color application, the Impressionists were the first of the moderns to make an important break with the simulative or representational tradition in Western painting. The academies had killed the spirit of this tradition to be sure. The Impressionists definitely broke from it and all later modern movements, most of all abstraction, were made possible by this violent cleavage.

The impressionist revolution produced two major reactions, both of which led to the twin poles of 20th century abstract art. Cézanne and Seurat, approaching the problem in quite different ways, sought to restore the formal qualities of things the Impressionists had abstracted and also to restore at the same time an architectural structure to the composition of a picture—a pictorial structure the Impressionists had often neglected in their light-struck, snap-shot view of landscape. Cézanne's and Seurat's investigations of form and picture-making carried them into a world of geometry. The first searched for the essence of all forms in nature in the sphere, the cylinder and the cone; the second stressed vertical, horizontal and angular lines of direction in his compositions, for structural and emotional purposes. Both were severely analytical in their geometrical observations and together they prepared the way quite logically for the cubist analysis of form initiated by Picasso and Braque. As regards representational subject matter, both Cézanne and Seurat carried forward the "denaturing" abstract tendencies of the Impressionists. By the very mathematical precision of Seurat's impressionist mosaic of color application he forced both animate and inanimate forms into a single pattern of existence, an existence firmly fixed within the four walls of his picture frame. He abstracted, as it were, the breath of life from the one and specific density from the other. By so doing, his landscapes, cabaret and circus scenes are sufficiently removed from representational reality to permit the observer to concentrate his

21

maximum attention upon the picture itself, its formal rhythms and color harmonies, with only a minimum associational interference called up by a ghostly, disembodied subject matter.

Cézanne advanced the dissolution of naturalistic representation still further. By attempting to penetrate to the essence of form in all its spatial implications in a portrait, landscape or still life he ended up by approaching the first two in exactly the same spirit as he approached the third. In effect, so determined, even labored, were his researches into the "realization" of form itself, eventually all things had to be abstracted from the natural world and dissected in his pictorial laboratory. A bowl of apples was as important to him as his wife or Mont Ste Victoire. The still life, in short, the lowest subject in the academic hierarchy became, with Cézanne, as important as any other. And by this very leveling process Cézanne practically negated the significance of all representational subject matter. This is the legacy, together with the sphere, the cylinder and the cone, he left to the Cubists and through them to the geometrical abstractionists.

Impressionist theory had a rational, pseudo-scientific basis. It owed much to the color researches of the chemist Chevreul and to Helmholz' researches into the properties of light. Monet, Pissarro and their fellows fought for their principles as painters. There are no overt indications in their peaceful landscapes that they were affected by the political, social or religious upheavals of their day.

During the 19th century France was torn by three revolutions, in 1830, 1848 and 1871. Europe as a whole throughout the century suffered many social and economic convulsions produced by the gigantic growth of industry and commerce and an equally gigantic growth in population. The Impressionists, however, and those rational explorers who followed them, Cézanne and Seurat, perhaps by their very denial of subject matter as such and particularly subject matter expressing any

GAUGUIN: *Goose-girl, Brittany*. 1888. Oil.
Collection Hunt Henderson, New Orleans

social significance, represent the optimistic spirit of rational inquiry which was one of the driving forces of the century. It was the same optimism that was capable of explaining away all the human wreckage produced by an irresponsible industrialism, the wanton use of child and female labor, not to speak of the cruel disregard of human life in the operation of increasingly dangerous machines. Perhaps, on the contrary, those artists who buried themselves in rational research into the problems of their art, by their very denial of the problems of society, and by living a life of retirement from these problems, thereby commented most forcefully, by their unconscious anarchism, on the state of the world as they found it.

There were artists who were unable to take this disinterested, rational course. Two of them, Gauguin and van Gogh, were actually so disillusioned they reacted violently against any rational exploration of the problems of picture making and in an evangelical spirit of reform turned to their own instincts and emotions as a basis for their art. In seeking to express themselves with all the emotional drive at their command, they burned themselves out in the process. Van Gogh out of his passionate child-like innocence forged a message in paint that is still a living force today. Gauguin, more sophisticated, tried with some success to recover an instinctive innocence of expression by emulating the art of primitive Breton and South Sea Island craftsmen. More important for this exposition, both artists "freed" color and form from any literal, imitative connotations and by this very deliverance from the double-edged "tyranny of the object," no less than by their insistence upon the value of instinctive emotion in artistic creation, they prepared the way, via the *fauve* painters and the German Expressionists, for the "free forms" and emotive color arrangements of the non-geometric, non-rational, expressionistic branch of abstract art.

Speaking very generally, I think it would be fair to say that the rationalist, in-

PICASSO: *Ma Jolie* (*Woman with a Guitar*). 1911-12. Oil.
The Museum of Modern Art,
acquired through the Lillie P. Bliss Bequest

tellectual rebels of the 19th century projected into the 20th century an impulse toward the abstract analysis of static, inanimate forms, the forms to be found in the still life. At any rate, they focused their experiments very largely on an examination of the still life, or landscape and figures reduced to still-life significance. The non-rationalist 19th century rebels, very significantly, I think, emphasized the emotive potentialities of a dynamic space, a space which for infinite permutations of emotional response and rhythmic vitality they found potentially greater in landscape than in still life. If this hypothetical delimitation of the problem of the evolution of art toward abstraction is accepted, I think we can better appreciate the development of the two branches of abstract art up to our own day. It is also a hypothesis that may help to keep our thinking straight as we plot our way through the maze of 20th century art movements, Cubism, Futurism, Orphism, Suprematism, Constructivism, Neo-Plasticism, Expressionism, Dada and Surrealism, all of which have had a direct or residual bearing on abstract art as we now find it today in America.

This may appear to be a fantastic over-simplification of a very complicated phenomenon. I confess to thinking, however, that if we don't attempt to use some basic measures, such as still life and landscape, the basic *content*, I am assuming, from which all abstract painting derives, the numerous art movements of this century become meaningless, technical gyrations not only in themselves but in relation to abstract art.

CUBISM AND FUTURISM

Before turning to the American scene, let us look first of all at two of the most important of all proto-abstract movements, Cubism and Futurism, both of which had a great influence here. Deriving, as we have said, from the researches of Cézanne and Seurat, the beginnings of Cubism date back to about 1908 under the twin aegis of Picasso and Braque. We must admit at once that however rational this movement was in the main, it began with and retained certain non-rational motivations. And here let us observe that the rational and non-rational currents in abstract art continually overlap.

In the case of Cubism, the primitivist, instinctual content of Gauguin's and van Gogh's paintings and the later discovery of the barbaric, expressive power of Negro sculpture played an important part in such an early cubist picture of Picasso's as his *Les Demoiselles d'Avignon*. And however much Picasso and his cubist followers tended to limit their researches to the still life, they never divorced themselves completely from the sentimental, even romantic, implications of their chosen subject matter—the paraphernalia of the studio, musical instruments, the guitar, mandolin and violin and the characters out of the old *commedia dell'arte* associated with such instruments, Harlequin, Columbine and Pierrot. Despite such emotional or non-rational elements in cubist painting, however, its rational motivation must still be said to have remained uppermost. It consisted in a process of analytical abstraction of several planes of an object to present a synthetic, simultaneous view of it. And by directing the formal planes of this synthetic view towards the observer rather than making them retreat by traditional perspective principles into an illusionistic space, the picture frame no longer acted as a window leading the eye into the distance but as a boundary enclosing a limited area of canvas or panel. In the so-called analytical

RUSSOLO: *Automobile* (Dynamism). 1913. Oil

DUCHAMP: *Nude Descending a Staircase*. 1912. Oil.
Louise and Walter Arensberg Collection, Hollywood

phase of Cubism, painting tended also to be monochromatic, presumably to avoid as
much as possible any sensuous or naturalistic reference to color. The leading Cubists, Picasso and Braque, refused to take abstraction further than this point and
actually in time climbed down from their pinnacle of analytical experiment to a more
decorative, sensuous plateau. They left the final step of total geometrical abstraction
to others.

Another proto-abstract movement, an anti-rational offshoot of Cubism, was
launched by the Italian Futurists about 1910. Rebelling against the cubist analysis
of static form, the Futurists were above all inspired by the dynamism of the machine,* which they proceeded to glorify and to make a central tenet in their artistic
credo. Man to the Futurist must accept the machine and emulate its ruthless power.
By way of emulation they attempted to paint movement by indicating abstract lines
of force (ill. p. 25) and schematic stages in the progress of a moving image. And
furthermore, in some instances they sought to involve the observer *in* their pictures
by viewing movement from an interior position—the inside of a trolley car, for
example—thus denying, as the Cubists did, formal laws of perspective. But where
the Cubists strove to eliminate three-dimensional space and thus bring the image in
the picture closer to the observer, although still at a distance, the Futurists at-

* Futurism is significantly a North Italian   the new industrial expansion in North Italy
movement and reflected in its machine worship   which took place in the early 1900s.

26

tempted to suck the observer into a pictorial vortex. The greatest difference between these two proto-abstract movements, however, is that the one, Cubism, is concerned with forms in static relationships while Futurism is concerned with them in a kinetic state. Furthermore, the Cubists, with few exceptions, paid no attention to the machine, as such, while the Futurists, as we have said, glorified it. The cubist movement, significantly, had no overt political implications and indulged in no manifestoes; the Futurists, on the other hand, worshipped naked energy for its own sake and in their writings pointed forward to the power-drunk ideology of Fascism. The Cubists, it may be said, immured themselves from any contact with the public by shutting themselves up in their studio laboratories. The Futurists came out into the market place and demagogically attempted to appeal to the man in the trolley car. If their pictures today seem dry and doctrinaire to some of us, the ideological appeal of Futurism and its political partner, Fascism, was, we are all uncomfortably aware, quite the reverse. Furthermore, the generally rational-minded Cubist contented himself as we have noted with the still-life materials of his studio for subject matter and abstract dissection, whereas the futurist picture falls mainly into the category of landscape and figure compositions, however urban and mechanical the emphasis.

These are the two movements, with more or less abstract tendencies, that first influenced the majority of experimental artists in this country, beginning about 1913 when both movements were at their height.

KUPKA: *Discs of Newton*. 1912. Oil. Owned by the artist

27

KANDINSKY: *Composition VII, Fragment I.* 1913. Oil.
The Museum of Modern Art,
acquired through the Lillie P. Bliss Bequest

THE BEGINNING OF ABSTRACT ART IN AMERICA—
THE ARMORY SHOW

The 1913 Armory Show gave the first great impetus toward abstraction in America.
It is perhaps not wholly a coincidence that this exhibition of upwards of 1600 paintings and sculpture should have been launched during a period of reform in American
politics. In 1912 the contest between Theodore Roosevelt and Wilson was a contest
between the reform wings of the Republican and Democratic parties. There was a
liberal, even radical spirit abroad in the land.* Ever since the Panic of 1907 "Big
Business" monopoly had been under fire. In art circles the monopolistic power of
the Academy was attacked by liberal-minded artists in the exhibition policy of the
newly formed Association of American Painters and Sculptors, set up to organize
an independent, unjuried, prizeless exhibition which eventually became the Armory
Show. The guiding spirits were Arthur B. Davies, president of the Association,
Walt Kuhn and Walter Pach—all of them painters. To fight the restrictive exhibition policies of the academic groups, these three and their supporters (there were
twenty-five members in the Association, including seven of the "ash-can" Eight)
decided to present a large exhibition of advance-guard foreign art, together with art
of a liberal tendency being produced here. The *Sonderbund* Exhibition in Cologne in
1912 and Roger Fry's two Grafton Galleries exhibitions in London in 1910 and 1912
were models for the New York show. Both London and Cologne had stressed

* Hutchins Hapgood, liberal writer, wrote in
the *New York Globe*, 1913, in an article entitled
"Art and Unrest": "We are living at a most
interesting moment in the art development of
America. It is no mere accident that we are also
living at a most interesting moment in the

political, industrial and social development of
America. What we call our 'unrest' is the condition of vital growth, and this beneficent
agitation is as noticeable in art and the woman's
movement as it is in politics and industry."

Cézanne, van Gogh and Gauguin as well as the advanced elements in the School of Paris. The Armory Show organizers went all out for every "extreme" expression then current in Paris. The shock to the American public and to American artists was tremendous and the howls of dismay from academic circles and conservative critics split the heavens. A reduced version of the exhibition was shown in Chicago and Boston. All told, the attendance amounted to about a quarter of a million. (Significantly enough for the history of abstract art in this country, the picture in the show that drew the greatest fire was Marcel Duchamp's cubist-futurist *Nude Descending a Staircase* (ill. p. 26). If any one picture can be said to have set the course of American abstract or proto-abstract painting, it is this one.)

The Years 1912-14 and the Rise of Many Abstract Art Movements in Europe

The Armory Show coincided in 1913 with one of the great highwater marks of advance-guard painting in Europe. Cubism and Futurism both reached a kind of apogee in that year and in their wake several Parisian and non-Parisian movements had, by 1913, carried art over to the most extreme abstract limits it has perhaps ever reached. The Parisian Orphists, Delaunay, the leader, Kupka (ill. p. 27), by association, and, related in intensified color abstraction, Picabia, by 1912 destroyed all that was left of the still-life subject matter in Picasso's and Braque's cubist compositions and restricted themselves to discs and planes of color in dynamic, geometrical relationships. The Paris-American Synchromists, Macdonald-Wright and Morgan Russell, an offshoot of the orphist movement, had their first large exhibitions in Munich and Paris in 1913. The Russian Kandinsky, one of the leaders of the German expressionist, Blue Rider group, by 1911 had arrived in his "improvisations" at an organic abstract "color music" which practically abandoned all traces of recognizable subject matter. His now famous book *The Art of Spiritual Harmony*, published in 1910, was translated into English in 1914 and had a wide influence on abstract theoretical thinking. (Translated excerpts appeared as early as 1912 in Stieglitz' *Camera Work*.) In Russia proper, three revolutionary artist groups, Suprematists, Non-Objectivists and Constructivists, all of them eventually associated with the later political revolution, turned to some of the most extreme

MALEVICH: *Fundamental Suprematist Elements*. 1913.
Pencil. The Museum of Modern Art

geometrical abstractions ever devised. Malevich, the leader of the Suprematists, by 1913 proposed a painting of a black square on a white ground as the final expression of abstract art. (By 1918, in his painting, *White on White*, he had carried even this Platonic geometrical logic to the absolute limit of non-objectiveness.) By 1913 Mondrian, the leading painter of what was later to be known as the *Stijl* group in Holland, had arrived, under Picasso's influence, at an extreme phase of geometrical Cubism. And eventually, of course, Mondrian led the way into what has ever since been the promised land of pure geometrical abstraction. In short, the years immediately preceding World War I have come to be associated with almost all the significant revolutionary art movements of this century.

Besides Seurat, Cézanne, van Gogh and Gauguin, the progenitors of cubist and expressionist abstraction, Picasso, Braque, Picabia, Kandinsky, Duchamp, Brancusi, Archipenko, Léger and many other cubist and abstract painters and sculptors were represented in the Armory Show and their influence is almost immediately apparent on advance-guard art in America during the First World War period. Such was the effect of this colossal, academy-shattering exhibition. In placing so much emphasis on its influence on anti-academic American artists, however, we must not be forgetful of certain pioneer artists and one important photographer who before 1913 had brought back from the Parisian revolutionary art center some of the fervor of discovery and protest that was later to culminate in the 69th Regiment Armory at Lexington Avenue and 25th Street. As early as 1898 Maurice Prendergast

MONDRIAN: *Composition in Grey, Blue, Yellow and Red.* 1921. Oil. Private collection

PICABIA: *The Dancer Star and her Dancing School.*
1913. Watercolor. Alfred Stieglitz Collection,
The Metropolitan Museum of Art, New York

had seen the work of Cézanne in Paris and began to spread his fame among his fellow Americans. Alfred Maurer, an early convert to the *Fauves*, Bernard Karfiol, Maurice Sterne, Max Weber and John Marin all had arrived in Paris by 1905 and their eyes were opened by such exhibitions as the first *fauve* pictures at the *Salon d'Automne* in that year and the exhibition of ten Cézannes at the same time, the second showing of the *Fauves* in 1906, together with ten more Cézannes (the year of his death), the Cézanne memorial exhibition in 1907 and the Gauguin retrospective in 1908. By this time, or shortly after, the number of American artists who were in Paris or had come and gone had greatly increased. Among the company were now Charles Demuth, Morgan Russell, Stanton Macdonald-Wright, Patrick Henry Bruce, Walter Pach, Arthur Dove, Andrew Dasburg, Morton Schamberg, Charles Sheeler, William and Marguerite Zorach, Marsden Hartley and, by way of Italy, Joseph Stella.

Perhaps most important of all for the modern movement as a whole in America and the abstract movement at least in part, Stieglitz, the American photographer, all-round enthusiast and impresario, set up shop at 291 Fifth Avenue in 1908 and proceeded to give first exhibitions in this country of Cézanne, Picasso, Brancusi, Matisse, Picabia, the futurist Severini, African Negro sculpture (as *art*) and many others. He was also the first to show the work of advance-guard Americans who had gone to Paris, among them Marin, Hartley, Macdonald-Wright and Dove, to name only four who are represented in the present exhibition. His "Younger American Artists" exhibition of 1910 was, in fact, the first modern group show in this country. His magazine *Camera Work*, first published in 1903, was the first art magazine in America to devote itself wholly to the modern movement. It is a tremendous record of pioneering achievement. And however much we may want to discount the somewhat mystic atmosphere engendered in Stieglitz' "291" gallery, the modern movement and, incidentally, the first years of abstract art in this country, will always be his debtor.

From 1913 to the present, abstract art in America has proceeded in two more or less distinct waves. The first wave, given its greatest impulse by the Armory Show, built up steadily through the World War I period and gradually lost its momentum about the mid '20s. The second wave began to rise in the early '30s. After a long, rather slow beginning it began to pick up speed in the mid '40s and appears now to be at its crest.

THE FIRST WAVE OF ABSTRACTION IN AMERICA, 1912—c.1925

The dominant trends during the World War I years were certainly cubist and futurist. Most of the paintings in the present exhibition dating from these first years reflect one or other or both of these importations. Not only were they the most sensational revolutionary movements in the Armory Show (despite the fact that the Futurists did not exhibit as a group), epitomized as we have seen in one picture that combined elements of both styles, Duchamp's *Nude Descending a Staircase* (p. 26), but the presence in America of such important foreign artists as Picabia, Duchamp and Gleizes immediately before and during the War years, undoubtedly had a good deal to do with setting the abstract pace at this time. Max Weber, who was in Matisse's first class in 1907, an intimate friend of the *douanier* Rousseau, and perhaps the most sympathetic and understanding student of all the Paris revolutions, was the most consistent Cubist of all the American artists of these early days. Yet even he tended to fuse with Cubism's static analysis of forms a dynamic, futurist element that is clearly revealed in the surging diagonals of his *New York*, 1912 (p. 37) and the *Rush Hour* (p. 38). More static, more cubist and, incidentally, more abstracted in their representational substructure are his *New York at Night* (p. 41) and *Chinese Restaurant* (p. 39). Perhaps the cold, intellectual, studio discipline that the analytical Cubism of Picasso and Braque demanded was too dry an exercise for Americans like Weber, Stella, Covert and Marin when faced with the speed and noise of America and particularly New York. In any case, I think it is significant that in the work of at least the first three, and to some extent Marin also, the Futurists' "lines of force," to reflect the movement of the industrial, mechanical age they worshipped, should play such an important role in the American abstract art of this time. To be sure, Stella was Italian-born and, when he returned to Italy in 1909, he not only came under the influence of his futurist compatriots, he actually exhibited with them before returning to America. His *Battle of Light, Coney Island* (p. 43), *Spring* (p. 42) and *Brooklyn Bridge* (p. 44) are the finest products of this futurist influence. Perhaps it is not too much to say that because of Stella's association with the vibrant new society that was America, its hopefulness together with its brutal industrial strength, his futurist essays have a more direct, pulsating vitality than is to be found in the painting of the native Futurists. The latter were too bound to a doctrinaire program that was as much a protest against what they considered the dead hand of their artistic past as an acceptance of a new industrial world.

Even in some of Feininger's work of this period, despite his over-all debt to Cubism, I think one can detect, particularly in such a picture as *Bridge V* (p. 45), a dynamic, futurist quality—diagonals and chevrons bursting beyond all four sides of the canvas—that is quite foreign to the static containment of the true cubist picture. Whether this dynamism is the result of Feininger's having seen some futurist painting, it would be hard to say. His long residence in Germany—and he was of course German by extraction—and his association there with the German Expressionists may have had much to do with the kaleidoscopic movement he injects into the formal body of Cubism.

Marsden Hartley, later a friend of Feininger, visited Paris first in 1912 and immediately came under the reigning cubist influence. However, for one reason or another, he soon found himself more at home in Germany and more in sympathy with the Blue Rider group of Expressionists, with whom he exhibited in Berlin in 1913. Under expressionist influence, and, one suspects, particularly that of Kandinsky, he too, like Feininger, broke with the cubist logic of static forms in a controlled, picture-bound space. His "*E*" (p. 51) and even the small *Abstraction* (p. 55) have an emotional verve and instinctive, intuitively derived rhythm of form and color that is foreign to Cubism. In the statement he wrote for the so-called Forum Exhibition held in New York in 1916 he appears to take issue with the rational, intellectual motivations of Cubism. "A fixed loathing of the imaginative has taken place," he says, and (perhaps revealing his disquiet with theoretical apologies for non-figurative abstraction—which he discontinued a few years after his return to America in 1916) he continues, "a continual searching for, or hatred of, subject matter is habitual, as if presence or absence of subject were a criterion." He then concludes cryptically: "It will be seen that my personal wishes lie in the strictly pictural notion, having observed much of this idea in the kinetic and the kaleidoscopic principles."

Man Ray was another American artist of these World War I years who, perhaps suffering as many did from the disillusionment that accompanies a war, rejected the rational basis of Cubism and fell under the spell of Duchamp's and Picabia's dadaist mockery of a machine-ridden, materialist civilization. He reduces his *Black Widow* (p. 56) and *The Rope Dancer Accompanies Herself with Her Shadows* (p. 57) to mechanistic, abstract cut-out images whose immateriality is made all the more striking by the spaceless, single plane on which they are conceived. And even in the *Aerograph* (p. 58) his drawing instruments have an eerie unreality that, while it may derive in part from the unsubstantial mist created by the airbrush (Man Ray was one of the first modern painters to use this technique) has also something to do with the undefined space in which the objects are suspended.

Equally indebted to Picabia's dadaist machine abstractions in technique, at least, Morton Schamberg, in contrast to Man Ray, avoids any dadaist mockery in his elegant reduction of quite recognizable and, again in contrast to dadaist practice, *workable* machine forms, to their essential geometrical outlines. However, in reducing the solid geometry of the machine to the plane geometry of the drawing board Schamberg arrives at a distinctive kind of machine abstraction that is unique with him. His friend Sheeler, by retaining suggestions of volume in his mechanical and architectural abstractions, is unable to achieve the absolute geometrical purity and a somewhat fantastic precision, that so distinguishes Schamberg's work at its best.

In all of the work we have discussed above it is noticeable that without exception, however disguised, dissected or distorted by cubist, futurist, expressionist or dadaist styles of abstraction the forms in the pictures may be, they are all more or less decipherable with reference to their natural or mechanical origins. The American painters who carried abstraction to a completely non-representational extreme were artists like Georgia O'Keeffe, Clifford Williams, Konrad Cramer, Abraham Walkowitz and, above all, the Synchromists, Macdonald-Wright and Morgan Russell, Andrew Dasburg, who was closely related to them in practice but whose work of this period has been destroyed, John Covert, partly futurist and partly dadaist in inspiration and Patrick Henry Bruce, who actually joined Delaunay's orphist movement, and was possibly influenced by Picabia's abstractions of 1913 and 1914. The Synchromists and Bruce were all Paris trained. The former, despite loud protestations at the time regarding the originality of their "movement," certainly owed much to the Orphists, who have a prior claim in point of time for the development of a "color music" presented in the form of pure abstract planes or discs in rhythmic, geometrical interplay. The Orphists were a splinter group which protested against the monochromatic tendencies of the Cubists proper together with the "impure" retention by the latter of recognizable subject matter. The American Synchromists, however indebted they may have been to the Orphists, succeeded in evolving a carefully worked-out program of color orchestration that so far as their theoretical exposition of it is concerned must be considered their own. As with the Orphists, hence their name, the Synchromists depended a good deal on the analogy of music for the justification of their pictures. Since both Macdonald-Wright and Russell published lucid statements describing their practice in the above-mentioned Forum Exhibition catalogue, the reader will better apprehend their intentions through direct quotations. Macdonald-Wright's contribution was as follows:

> I strive to divest my art of all anecdote and illustration, and to purify it to the point where the emotions of the spectator will be wholly aesthetic, as when listening to good music.
>
> Since plastic form is the basis of all enduring art, and since the creation of intense form is impossible without color, I first determined, by years of color experimentation, the relative spatial relation of the entire color gamut. By placing pure colors on recognizable forms (that is, by placing advancing colors on advancing objects, and retreating colors on retreating objects), I found that such colors destroyed the sense of reality, and were in turn destroyed by the illustrative contour. Thus, I came to the conclusion that color, in order to function significantly,

must be used as an *abstract medium*. Otherwise the picture appeared to me merely as a slight, lyrical decoration.

Having always been more profoundly moved by pure rhythmic form (as in music) than by associative processes (such as poetry calls up), I cast aside as nugatory all natural representation in my art. However, I still adhered to the fundamental laws of composition (placements and displacements of mass as in the human body in movement), and created my pictures by means of color-form which, by its organization in three dimensions, resulted in rhythm.

Later, recognizing that painting may extend itself into time, as well as be a simultaneous presentation, I saw the necessity for a formal climax which, though being ever in mind as the final point of consummation, would serve as a *point d'appui* from which the eye would make its excursions into the ordered complexities of the picture's rhythms. Simultaneously my inspiration to create came from a visualization of abstract forces interpreted, through color juxtapositions, into terms of the visual. In them was always a goal of finality which perfectly accorded with my felt need in picture construction.

By the above one can see that I strive to make my art bear the same relation to painting that polyphony bears to music. Illustrative music is a thing of the past: it has become abstract and purely aesthetic, dependent for its effect upon rhythm and form. Painting, certainly, need not lag behind music.

Morgan Russell's statement follows:

My first synchromies represented a personal manner of visualizing by color rhythms; hence my treatment of light by multiple rainbow-like color-waves which, expanding into larger undulations, form the general composition.

In my next step I was concerned with the elimination of the natural object and with the retention of color rhythms. An example of this period is the *Cosmic Synchromy*. The principal idea in this canvas is a spiralic plunge into space, excited and quickened by appropriate color contrasts.

In my latest development I have sought a "form" which, though necessarily archaic, would be fundamental and permit of steady evolution, in order to build something at once Dionysian and architectural in shape and color.

Furthermore I have been striving for a greater intensity of pictorial aspect. In the Middle Ages cathedral organs were louder than the sounds then heard in life; and men were made to feel the order in nature through the dominating ordered notes of the organ. But to-day the chaotic sounds and lights in our daily experience are intenser than those in art. Therefore art must be raised to the highest intensity if it is to dominate life and give us a sense of order.

Much has been said concerning the rôle of intellect in painting. Common-sense teaches that the mind's analytic and synthetic powers, like vigorous draughts of fresh air, kill the feeble and invigorate the strong. The strong assimilate the suggestions of reason to their creative reactions: the feeble superimpose reason on their pictures, thus petrifying their work and robbing it of any organic unity. This unity is a necessity to all great art and results only from a creative vision handling the whole surface with supple control.

I infuse my own vitality into my work by means of my sense of relations and adjustments. The difference between a picture produced by precise formulas and one which is the result of *sensibilité*, is the difference between a mechanical invention and a living organism.

While there will probably always be illustrative pictures, it cannot be denied that this century may see the flowering of a new art of forms and colors alone. Personally, I believe that non-illustrative painting is the purest manner of aesthetic expression, and that, provided the basic demands of great composition are adhered to, the emotional effect will be even more intense than if there were present the obstacle of representation. Color is form; and in my attainment of abstract form I use those colors which optically correspond to the spatial extension of the forms desired.

After reading these statements the reader may suspect that the synchromist movement, if two men can be said to form a movement, was almost too rationally conceived, too verbally programmatic, too rarified to be able to sustain the emotional requirements of the artists themselves or the continued interest of the observer. In fact, Synchromism had a relatively short life and by about 1919-20 it had lost its significance and both Macdonald-Wright and Russell returned to figurative painting which they have continued ever since.

It is perhaps significant that with the death of Synchromism towards the end of World War I there appears to be a marked tapering off of abstract tendencies as a whole. The first fine flurry of excitement created by the Armory Show had spent itself, and as we move into the decade of the '20s, there is a noticeable decline in the number of artists following the extremist explorations in any one of the abstract directions mentioned above. Actually, the abstract cause as a whole may be said to have been weakened by the defection in the '20s of many of its doughtiest practitioners. In addition to the demise of the Synchromists as a "movement," Weber and Hartley both abandoned their geometrical and expressionist abstract essays and devoted themselves to other interests, more or less representational by contrast. John Covert gave up art altogether and became a business man in 1923. Schamberg died in 1918. The only new convert of note was Stuart Davis and while he has since become one of the mainstays of a kind of cubist-derived, geometrical abstraction and has held consistently to an abstract course to this day, his addition to the ranks in 1921 can hardly be said to have made up for the leavetaking of so many of the older leaders. Against this general weakening of the abstract current, however, the foundation of the *Société Anonyme* in 1920 by Katherine Dreier, Marcel Duchamp and Man Ray, devoted as it was to the collection and exhibition of many phases of abstract art, both foreign and American, did more than any other single instrumentality in helping the abstract movement here to become entrenched and in furthering and encouraging its progress. While the general decline in interest in cubist-abstract art here in the '20s may well reflect a similar decline in interest in Paris at the same time and a corresponding increase in interest in a new movement, Surrealism, officially announced by André Breton in 1924, the *Société Anonyme* between the '20s and the '40s did much to hold the abstract fort.

WEBER: *New York*. 1912. Oil, 40 x 32″. Collection Wright Ludington

WEBER: *Rush Hour, New York*. 1915. Oil, 36¼ x 30¼″. Owned by the artist

WEBER: *Chinese Restaurant.* 1915. Oil, 40 x 48″. The Whitney Museum of American Art. *Not in the exhibition.*

WEBER: *New York at Night.* 1915. Oil, 34½ x 22″. A. P. Rosenberg & Co., Inc.

STELLA: *Battle of Light, Coney Island*. 1914. Oil, 6′ 3¾″ x 7′. Yale University Art Gallery, *Société Anonyme* Collection

OPPOSITE: STELLA: *Spring*. 1914. Oil, 75 x 40⅛″. Yale University Art Gallery, *Société Anonyme* Collection

Stella: *Brooklyn Bridge.* 1917-18. Oil, 7′ x 6′ 4″. Yale University Art Gallery, *Société Anonyme* Collection

Opposite above: Feininger: *Bridge V.* 1919. Oil, 31¾ x 39⅝″. Buchholz Gallery

Opposite: Feininger: *Zirchow VII.* 1918. Oil, 31½ x 39½″. Owned by the artist

MARIN: *Tree Forms*. 1915. Watercolor, 14⅛ x 16⅜". Collection Charles Alan

MARIN: *Lower Manhattan* (*Composing Derived from Top of Woolworth*). 1922. Watercolor, 21⅝ x 26⅞″. The Museum of Modern Art, acquired through the Lillie P. Bliss Bequest

COVERT: *Temptation of St. Anthony.*
1916. Oil, 25¾ x 23¾″.
Yale University Art Gallery,
Société Anonyme Collection

PACH: *St. Patrick's at Night.*
1916. Oil, 18 x 24″.
Owned by the artist

COVERT: *Brass Band*. 1919. Oil and string on board, 26 x 24″. Yale University Art Gallery, *Société Anonyme* Collection

Morgan Russell: *Synchromy To Form*. 1913-14. Oil, 11′ 3″ x 10′ 3″. Owned by the artist

HARTLEY: "*E*." 1915. Oil, 47½ x 47½". The estate of the artist, courtesy of A. P. Rosenberg & Co., Inc.

BRUCE: *Composition II*. Before 1918. Oil, 38¼ x 51″. Yale University Art Gallery, *Société Anonyme* Collection

MACDONALD-WRIGHT: *Conception Synchromy*. 1916.
Oil, 66 x 24". Earl Stendhal Gallery

MACDONALD-WRIGHT: *Synchromy*. 1917.
Oil, 31 x 24″. The Museum of Modern Art,
given anonymously

HARTLEY: *Abstraction*. c. 1916. Oil, 13¼ x 16¼″.
Collection Mr. and Mrs. Hudson Walker, courtesy
the University Gallery, University of Minnesota

Man Ray: *Black Widow*. 1915.
Oil, 70 x 34". Owned by the artist

Man Ray: *The Rope Dancer Accompanies Herself with Her Shadows.* 1916. Oil, 52 x 73⅜″. State University of Iowa

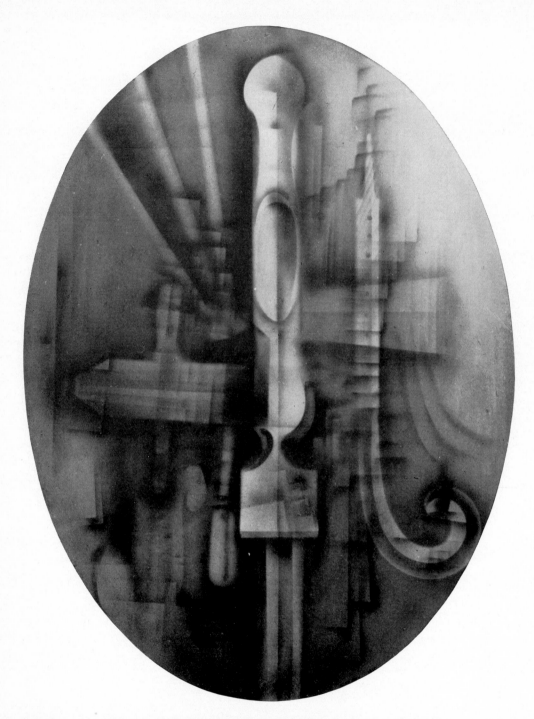

MAN RAY: *Aerograph*. 1919. Airbrush and watercolor, 27 x 20″. Owned by the artist

ᴇɪᴇʀ: *Abstract Portrait of Marcel Duchamp*. 1918. Oil, 18 x 32″. The Museum of Modern Art, Mrs. John D. Rockefeller, Jr.
rchase Fund

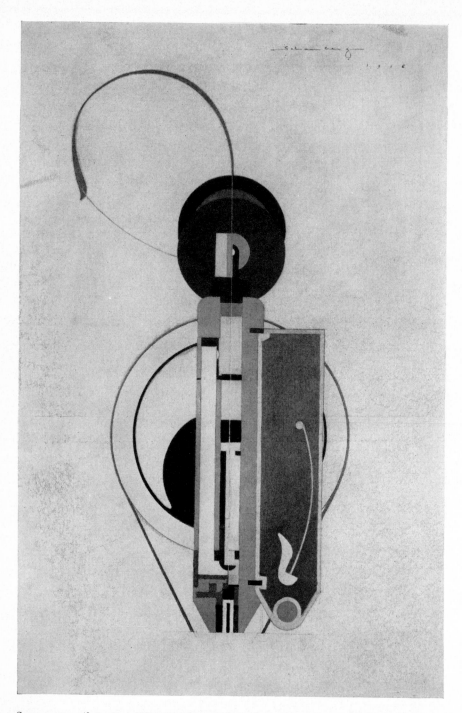

SCHAMBERG: *Abstraction*. 1916. Oil, 30 x 20¼″. Louise and Walter Arensberg Collection

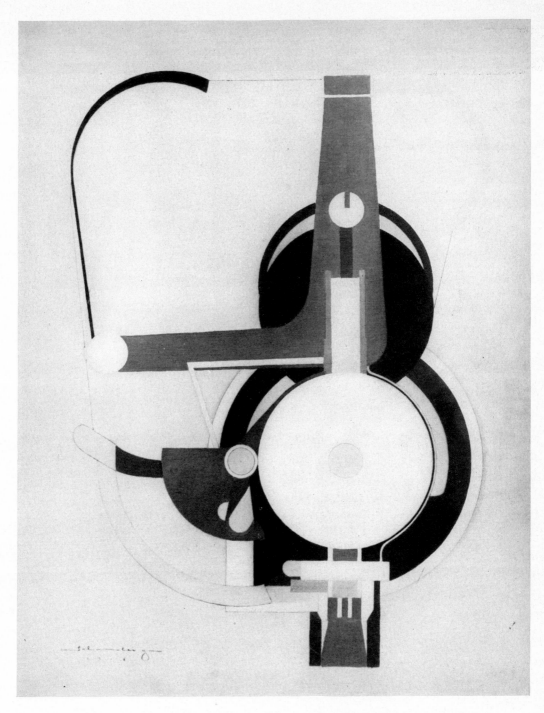

SCHAMBERG: *Machine*. 1916. Oil, 30⅛ x 22¾″. Yale University Art Gallery, *Société Anonyme* Collection

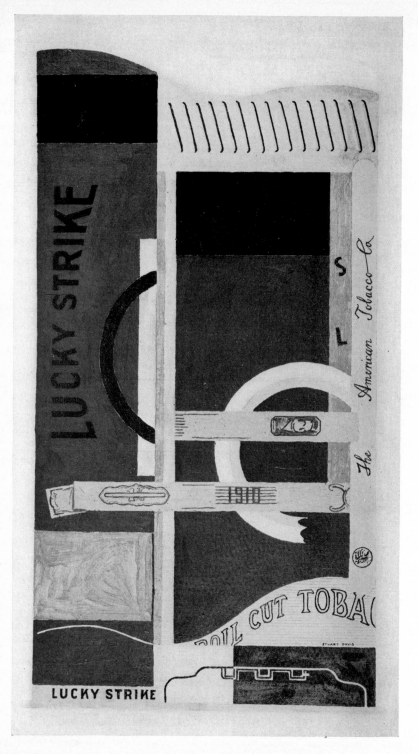

Davis: *Lucky Strike.* 1921. Oil, 33⅛ x 18″. The Downtown Gallery

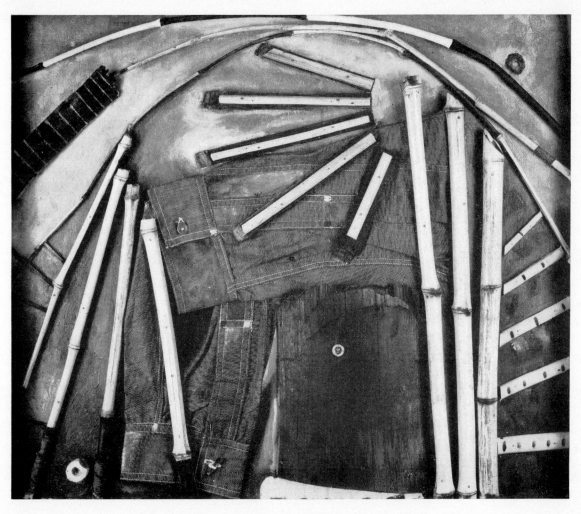

Dove: *Goin' Fishin'*. c. 1925. Collage, 19½ x 24″. The Phillips Gallery

THE SECOND WAVE OF ABSTRACTION, C. 1930-1950

During the years of economic depression and threats of war in the '30s the abstract wave in America, if such it can be called, was relatively weak and unimportant compared with the tremendous swell of American Scene and Social Realist painting which accompanied the hysteria and social convulsions of these tragic days. Nevertheless, despite the contrary directions of much of the government-supported art of the time, there were a few American artists who like Davis, Dove and Carles continued along their several abstract paths and a number who turned anew to abstract problems.

Once again, as with the pioneers of 1913, American abstractionists looked to Europe for inspiration. Meanwhile, the old opposition between emotional Expressionism and rational, geometrical Cubism had since 1913 resolved itself into related polarities of surrealist explorations of the subconscious, "automatic" painting, the evocation of dream imagery on the one hand and on the other, of a geometrical abstract movement, rational, architectural, almost mathematical in its purity of purpose, the culmination of similar tendencies in Russia (Suprematism and Constructivism), France (Purism), Holland (*de Stijl*) and Germany (the Bauhaus). The Surrealists were an outgrowth of the Dadaists and retained much of their mocking irrationalism. The geometrical abstractionists of the '30s were the Russian pioneers like Pevsner and Gabo, exiles from the original movements in revolutionary Russia:

GABO: *Monument for an Airport*. 1924-25. Glass and metal. Owned by the artist

Mondrian and van Doesburg and other members of the *Stijl* movement in Holland, founded in 1917, whose interests encompassed not only painting but architecture and typography; the Bauhaus group in Germany, founded during the Weimar Republic, who drew inspiration both from Russia and Holland; and the French Purists, led by Le Corbusier and Ozenfant, who revolted in 1916 against the decorative prettiness of post-1914 Cubism.

It is worth noting again that Surrealism was an anarchistic revolt of individuals against what they considered to be the dead weight of a rational, technologically enslaved society. The geometrical abstractionists, on the other hand—whatever their nationality—were without exception motivated by a desire to control the machine and to use it in the interests of the masses of mankind. The Surrealists were essentially a literary group and only secondarily painters and sculptors. The geometrical abstractionists looked again, after a long period of neglect, at engineering as the new mistress of the arts and from her derived confirmation of their interest in the plane and solid geometry of space and volume, originally inspired by Cubism. It should further be noted that within the ranks of the evangelical geometricists there was room—or at least there was at the Bauhaus—for a romantic, cubist-expressionist like Feininger or a discreet explorer of the unconscious like Klee. This may explain the greater variety of abstract styles that relate themselves to the geometricists as a group. The compulsive Surrealist, on the contrary, is antipathetic to a geometric austerity. Drawing often from the visceral regions of his subconscious, his imagery is organically shaped and "realistically" colored by its intestinal and venous sources. The picture space enclosing this imagery is always of an indefinite, suggestive kind. The geometricists, in their purest state at least, look beyond the human body to a lucid, even austere architectural and mechanical world of usually rectangular shapes and primary colors, severely prescribed in a geometrically contained and essentially impalpable, abstract space.

Among the early motivating factors here in America for the acceptance of these two points of view, the universal social and economic unrest of the '30s is undoubtedly of primary importance. The Depression, which was not restricted to America; the rise of the Nazis in 1933 and the disbandment of the Bauhaus faculty (some of whom like Gropius, Breuer, Moholy-Nagy, Feininger and Albers eventually came to this country); disillusionment with chauvinistic tendencies in American Scene painting; the inadequacy and sentimentality of most of the Social Realist painters; the publication in English of cogent books and catalogues such as Herbert Read's *Art Now* (1933), James Johnson Sweeney's *Plastic Redirections in 20th Century Painting* (1934), Alfred Barr's *Cubism and Abstract Art* (1936) and his *Fantastic Art, Dada, Surrealism* (1936); the opening of A. E. Gallatin's Gallery of Living Art at New York University in 1927; the founding of the Museum of Modern Art in 1929 and its exposition of abstract and surrealist art in connection with Barr's books; the retrospective exhibition of American Abstract Painting at the Whitney Museum in 1935; the organization of the American Abstract Artists group in 1936; the publication in 1937 of an *International Survey of Constructive Art* by the *Circle* group in

65

England; the foundation of the Museum of Non-Objective Painting in 1937; the coming to America of Mondrian in 1940; all these, and many more, contributing factors encouraged a growing number of artists, aside from their personal desires, to take up an abstract direction.

From artists' statements published in American Abstract Artists catalogues of 1938 and 1939, one gathers that a majority of the exhibitors in those pre-war years may have been moved to take up abstract art as a positive answer to the chaotic Depression years. George L. K. Morris may take a purely aesthetic line in his demand that abstract artists must "strip art inward to those very bones from which all cultures take their life" and he points to Minoan sculpture and early Chinese bronzes as exemplars of abstract art in the past. Alice Mason, another contributor, however, insists that the abstract artist "breaks with the past and looks into a new experimental world." Rosalind Bengelsdorf also sees in a brave new world of science a justification for abstract art. "It is the era of science and the machine," she says, " . . . . . . so-called abstract painting is the expression in art of this age. The abstract painter coordinates his emotional temptations with his reason: the reason of this age." Ibram Lassaw also turns his back on the past. "Our own age," he says, "in some ways so completely different from all past times and at the same time so eclectic of our heritage, is now forming a new viewpoint of art."

It is some such attitude of optimism and hope for a new scientific age (recalling the rational experimenters of the 19th century) that may explain in part the plane and solid geometrical approach of most of the abstract artists of the '30s, many of whom have continued in the same vein until today. It helps to explain, too, the interest of some of the painters and all of the sculptors in new materials and technical methods, for example new chemical colors, plastics and metal cutting and welding.

As against the geometric abstractionists, there were a few artists in the '30s such as Gorky (p. 126), Calder (p. 108), Lassaw (p. 131) and Smith (p. 110) who looked mainly to the surrealist inspiration of Miro and Picasso for their organic abstractions. With the latter three sculptors there is probably to be seen a fusion of something of the constructivist spirit with surrealist fantasy. But Gorky consistently explored the labyrinthine, automatic, dream writing of the Surrealists in a breathing, non-geometric space (pp. 126, 127). And it is from these surrealist-inspired, organic abstractionists of the '30s that many of the post-World War II abstractionists derive. This whole anti-intellectual, expressionist school, like its earlier forbears van Gogh, Gauguin, Kandinsky and others, appeared to express its evangelical disgust with a dislocated world of wars and depressions by a return to an emotionally inspired imagery and spatial dynamism, in an anarchistic effort to throw off the constrictions of worn-out traditions, whether social, religious or artistic.

To return to our original hypothesis in which we related the still life and inanimate architectural and mechanical artifacts to the geometrical abstract impulse, and the dynamic space and organic shapes of landscape to the expressionist compulsion, these two polarities of approach are still in evidence in the two major abstract schools in America. Simply stated, I am aware that this hypothesis is open to objec-

66

Miro: *Dog Barking at a Kite.* c. 1935. Oil.
Private collection, New York

tion and qualifications. It is quite possible, of course, to present a still life in a dynamic space and landscape in a static one. The fact remains, however, that the still life by the very limitations or enclosures of space within which it is usually conceived lends itself better to a static, geometrical analysis of forms. The very term still life, or better, the French equivalent *nature morte*, implies a quality of static space that is foreign to the expansive, indefinite spatial extension of landscape. Very significantly, I think, particularly in relation to the history of the two current abstract movements in America, the geometric abstractionists, tied as I suggest they are to a *nature morte* conception, find it practically impossible to base their abstractions on the human figure. The still life has always implied the absence of the human figure. Landscape, on the contrary, has often included it both as a measure of scale and as an emotive component in the universal scene to which landscape may refer. It is surely additionally significant that the Surrealists, to whom our expressionist abstractionists owe a considerable debt, while they did not limit themselves to dream landscapes, nevertheless emphasized them to a great extent. They also revived an interest in the human figure both as a total entity and in a dissected, disjointed, even intestinal state. The expressionist abstractionists have retained the expansive spatial freedom of the Surrealists, one may say, together with the "free forms" derived from living organisms in contrast to still life. Furthermore, the Expressionists by their very preoccupation with organic tensions, however abstract their forms may be, imply, at least empathically, a human relationship and in a few isolated examples, in fact, they are beginning to experiment with the human figure as a recognizable entity. In this connection, it might be added parenthetically that the reason for the much smaller proportion of abstract sculpture to abstract painting in Amer-

67

ica, and elsewhere, is explained by the continued acceptance of the human figure as a basis of expression by the majority of modern sculptors.

I think one can say finally, reverting to our original argument, that the protest of the geometric abstractionists against conditions of social and economic chaos is given a positive answer in their clean, orderly constructions. The Expressionists, on the contrary, look not to architecture or the machine for salvation. In an intense spirit of self-examination that borders often on the mystical, they appear to be seeking to uncover the primal responses of the human organism to its environment. Only thus, they seem to say, can man and his art be reborn and again attain a state of grace.

* * * * * * *

Because of their number and variety, I have found it necessary to group the paintings and sculpture here illustrated under five different headings. These categories may at times appear arbitrary and some of the works included under one head undoubtedly show correspondence with another. However, since it is impossible here to discuss so many works individually, I hope the artists concerned will forgive me for dragooning them into one or other company and that the reader's interests will be better served by a systematic catalogue of illustrations, however distorted it may be in certain instances.

The categories I have set up are:
1. Pure Geometric
2. Architectural and Mechanical Geometric
3. Naturalistic Geometric
4. Expressionist Geometric
5. Expressionist Biomorphic

The first two are definitely cubist-constructivist in derivation; the third is mainly cubist and expressionist in origin; the fourth and fifth are called Expressionist for want of a more precise word. It is possible to substitute the term Surrealist but I think this would be inexact. Using the term Expressionist in its traditional sense to mean a combination of the unrational, irrational, symbolic, fantastic and self-expressive, its link with Surrealism is sufficiently clear.

The following groups of illustrations are preceded by explanatory notes outlining what I think are the characteristics of each category. These notes should be read as summaries in the light of this essay as a whole.

PURE GEOMETRIC (*pp. 69-84*)

CHARACTERISTICS:

   a. Pure rectangular or curvilinear forms bearing no recognizable relationships to natural forms; statically contained within the picture frame.

   b. With few exceptions, space is treated two-dimensionally in painting and by a geometrical schematization in the sculpture constructions.

ORIGINS: Cubism, Constructivism, *de Stijl*, Bauhaus.

MORRIS: *Concretion*. 1936. Oil, 54¾ x 70½". The Downtown Gallery

FERREN: *Composition on Green*. 1936. Oil, 28¾ x 39″. Owned by the artist

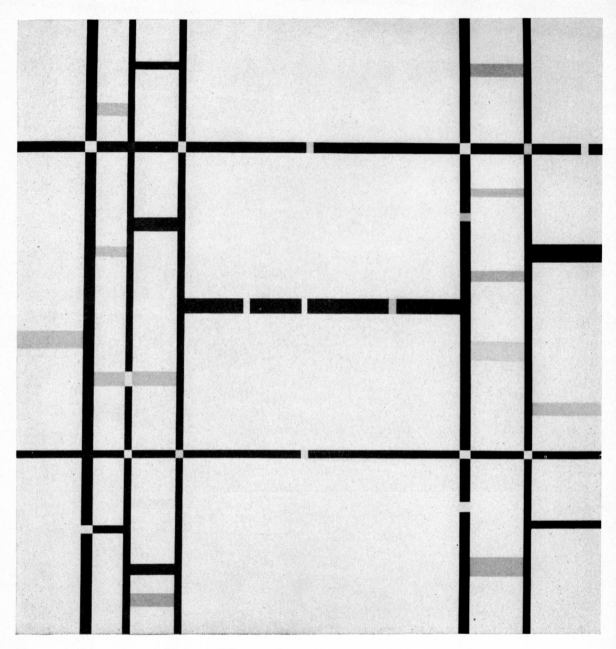

DILLER: *Composition*. 1943-44. Oil, 42 x 42″. Pinacotheca Gallery

GLARNER: *Relational Painting.* 1947-48. Oil, 43⅛ x 42¼″. The Museum of Modern Art, Purchase Fund.

Cavallon: *Abstraction*. 1950. Oil, 36 x 42". Egan Gallery

ALBERS: *Dark*. 1947. Oil, 26½ x 38″. Sidney Janis Gallery

PEREIRA: *Composition in White*. 1942. Mixed medium on parchment, 18 x 18″. The Newark Museum

HOLTY: *Equestrian*. 1942. Oil, 54 x 36″. Kootz Gallery

MORRIS: *Suspended Discs*. 1950. Oil, 23 x 19″. The Downtown Gallery

GALLATIN: *Forms*. 1949-50. Oil, 30 x 23″. Pinacotheca Gallery

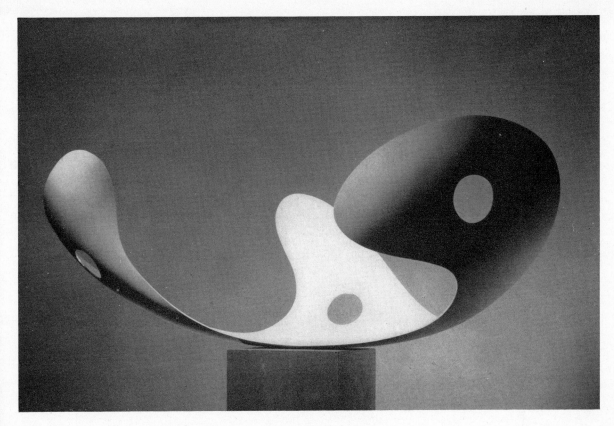

DE RIVERA: *Yellow Black*. 1946-47. Aluminum, 60″ long. Mortimer Levitt Gallery

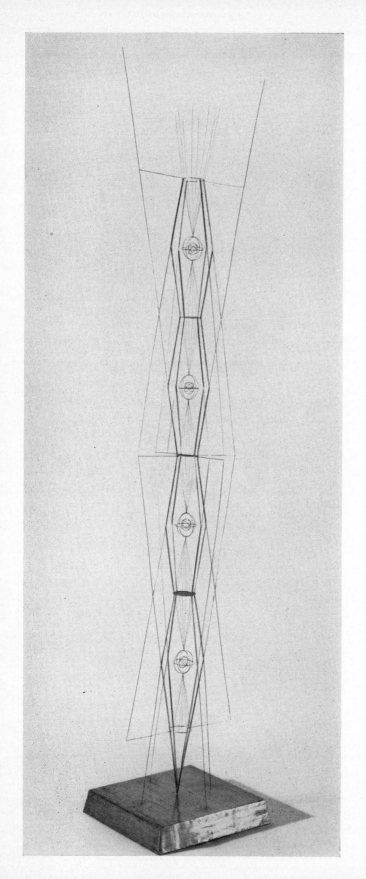

LIPPOLD: *Primordial Figure.* 1947.
Copper and brass, 8′ 1″ high.
Collection Mrs. William A. Pedlar

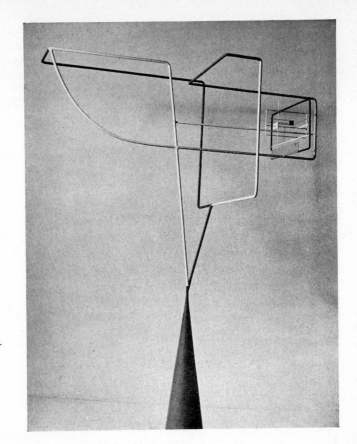

ROSZAK: *Spatial Construction*. 1943.
Steel wire and wood, painted, 23¼ ″ high.
Pierre Matisse Gallery

ROSZAK: *Construction in White*. 1940.
Painted wood and plastic, 36 x 36 ″.
Pierre Matisse Gallery

FULLER: *String Construction in Yellow and Grey*. 1946. String, 30 x 24″. Bertha Schaefer Gallery

ARCHITECTURAL AND MECHANICAL GEOMETRIC *(pp. 85-91)*

a. Rectangular or curvilinear forms derived from recognizable architectural or mechanical prototypes; statically contained within the picture frame.

b. Space treated two-dimensionally (with one exception, p. 89).

ORIGINS: Cubism, Constructivism, *de Stijl*, Bauhaus.

Balcomb Greene: *Blue Space*. 1941. Oil, 20 x 30″. Bertha Schaefer Gallery

SPENCER: *Two Bridges*. 1947. Oil, 28½ x 45½″. Collection Mr. and Mrs. Roy R. Neuberger.

LEWANDOWSKI: *Christmas Tree*. 1950. Oil, 40 x 22″. The Downtown Gallery

MODEL: *Uptown*. 1947. Oil, 62 x 47". Sidney Janis Gallery

CRAWFORD: *From the Bridge.* 1942. Oil, 28 x 40¼". The Downtown Gallery

NATURALISTIC GEOMETRIC (*pp. 92-101*)

CHARACTERISTICS:

a. Recognizable natural or architectural forms whose geometrical structure has been emphasized in themselves and in relation to each other.

b. Space treated three-dimensionally and often with atmospheric implications.

ORIGINS: Cubism, Expressionism, Constructivism.

DOVE: *Sand Barge.* 1930. Oil, 30 x 40″. The Phillips Gallery

DOVE: *Rising Tide*. 1944. Oil, 27 x 36″. The Downtown Gallery

O'KEEFFE: From the *Pelvis Series*. 1947. Oil, 39¾ x 48″. Owned by the artist

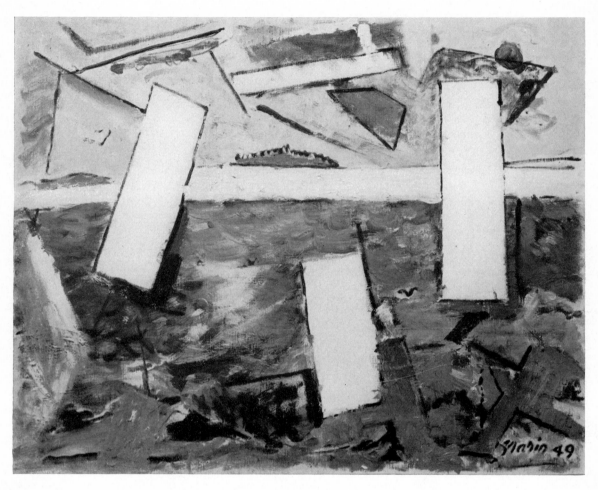

MARIN: *The Fog Lifts*. 1949. Oil, 22 x 28″. The Downtown Gallery

FEININGER: *Vita Nova*. 1947. Oil, 31½ x 39½". Buchholz Gallery

CALLAHAN: *Abstraction I.* 1950. Tempera, 20 x 24¼". Maynard Walker Gallery

COGGESHALL: *Nightscape.* 1950. Oil, 27 x 48″. Betty Parsons Gallery

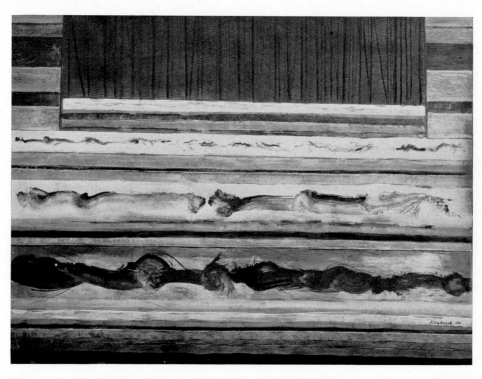

KIENBUSCH: *Low Tide.* 1950. Gouache, 22½ x 31″. Kraushaar Galleries

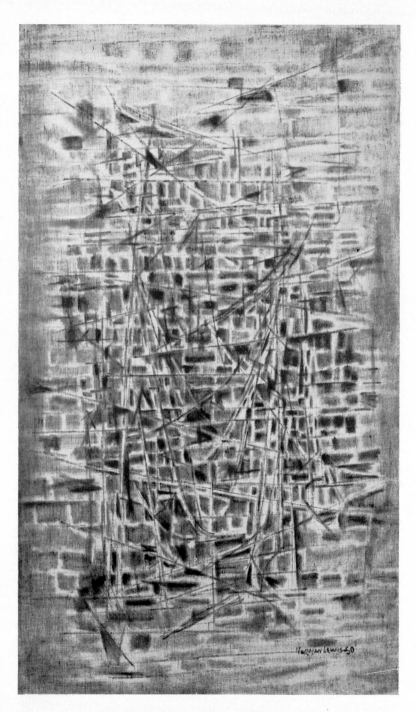

LEWIS: *Urban*. 1950. Oil, 50 x 29¾″. Willard Gallery

MORGAN: *Mediterranean Night*. 1949. Oil, 10⅜ x 15½″. J. B. Neumann Gallery

HELIKER: *Scava*. 1950. Oil, 11½ x 18″. Collection American Academy of Arts and Letters, Childe Hassam Purchase Fund

EXPRESSIONIST GEOMETRIC (*pp. 102-124*)

CHARACTERISTICS:

   a. Rectangular and curvilinear forms arranged usually in dynamic, organic relationships, but with an over-all geometrical control to the composition.

   b. Space usually treated three-dimensionally and often in a vibrant, pulsating manner, reflecting the inward and outward tensions and thrusts of the forms within the space.

ORIGINS: Cubism, Expressionism, Dada, Surrealism.

KNATHS: *Maritime.* 1931. Oil, 40 x 32″. The Phillips Gallery

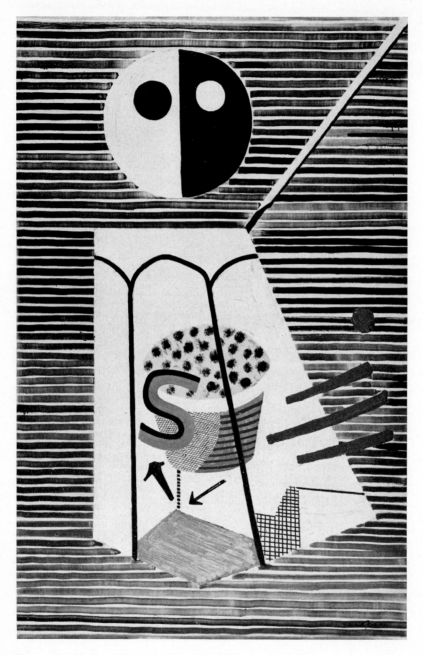

DAVIS: *Salt Shaker*. 1931. Oil, 49⅞ x 32″. Collection Mrs. Edith Gregor Halpert

OPPOSITE: DAVIS: *For Internal Use Only*. 1945. Oil, 45 x 28″. The Miller Company Collection "Painting Toward Architecture"

BROWNE: *Variations on a Still Life*. 1938. Oil, 47 x 36″. Grand Central Moderns Gallery

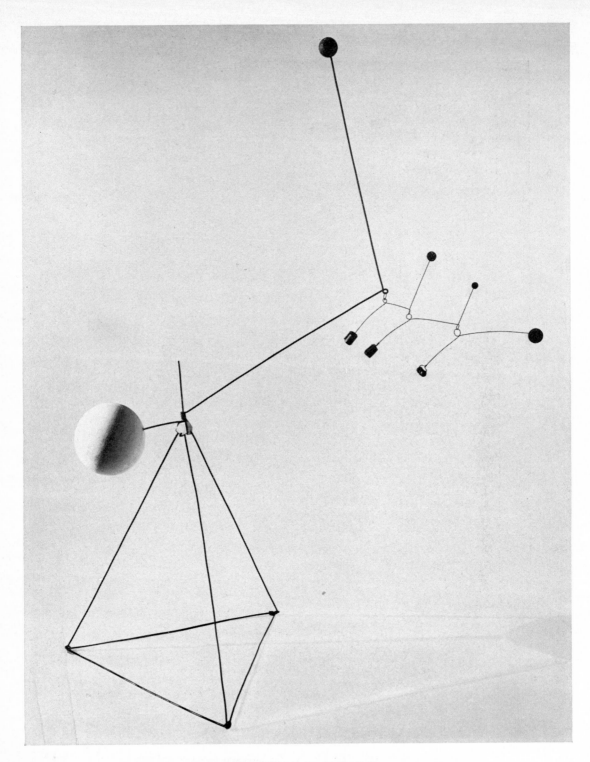

CALDER: *Feathers*. 1931. Wood, steel rod, lead, 39½″ high. Buchholz Gallery

CALDER: *Spiny*. 1942. Sheet aluminum, painted, 26″ high. Buchholz Gallery

SMITH: *Amusement Park*. 1937. Steel with cadmium, 33¾″ long. Willard Gallery

<small>Calder:</small> *Gypsophila II*. 1950. Metal and wire, painted, 54″ high. Buchholz Gallery

112

REINHARDT: *No. 11*. 1949. Oil, 50 x 20″.
Betty Parsons Gallery

OPPOSITE: TOMLIN: *No. 7*. 1950. Oil,
6′ 8″ x 3′ 10″. Betty Parsons Gallery

MOTHERWELL: *Western Air*. 1946-47. Oil, 72 x 54″. The Museum of Modern Art, Purchase Fund

Ruvolo: *Undulating Landscape.* 1950.
Oil, 30 x 43¾″. Catherine Viviano Gallery

Ryan: *No. 8.* 1950. Collage, 15¾ x 12½″.
The Museum of Modern Art, Purchase Fund

GOLUBOV: *Fantasy*. 1945. Oil, 30 x 46″. Artists' Gallery

Ferren: *Painting.* 1950. Oil, 22 x 30″.
Owned by the artist

McNeil: *Abstraction.* 1949. Oil, 30 x 24″.
Egan Gallery

ALFRED RUSSELL: *Rue Saint Denis*. 1948-50. Oil, 54 x 40″. Peridot Gallery

Conover: *Gray Abstraction*. 1949. Oil, 51 x 30″. Laurel Gallery

HOFMANN: *The Window*. 1950. Oil, 48 x 35¾″. The Metropolitan Museum of Art, gift of Mr. and Mrs. Roy R. Neuberger

JIMMY ERNST: *A Time for Fear.* 1949. Oil, 23⅞ x 20″.
The Museum of Modern Art, Katharine Cornell Fund

SHAW: *Force in Space.* 1950. Oil, 48 x 32″.
Passedoit Gallery

KENT: *Presence*. Magnesite, 43¾″ high.
Betty Parsons Gallery

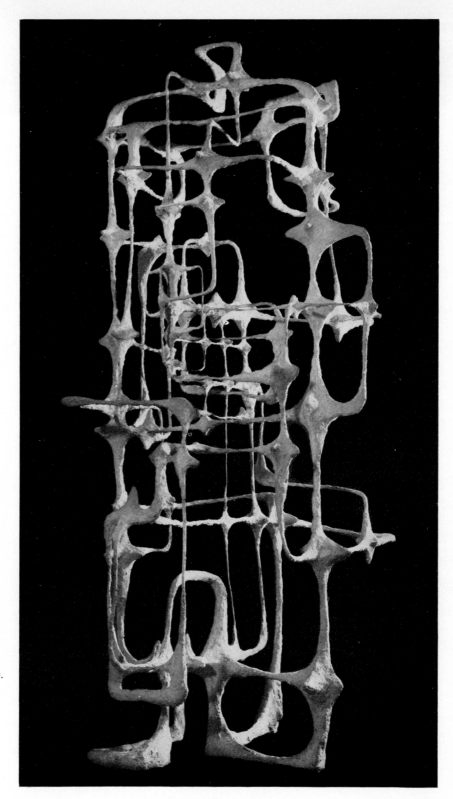

LASSAW: *The Milky Way:*
A Polymorphic Space. 1950.
Plastic metal, 51½″ high.
Owned by the artist

FERBER: *The Bow.* 1950. Lead, 48″ high. Betty Parsons Gallery

EXPRESSIONIST BIOMORPHIC (*pp. 125-147*)

CHARACTERISTICS:

a. Irregular-shaped forms and calligraphic interlacings bearing, if any, a relation to organic or anatomical forms; composed usually in dynamic, symbolic or emotively suggestive relationships; often showing evidence of an automatist or "doodling" origin.

b. Space treated three-dimensionally; in its variegated depths, shallows and movement related to concepts of space found in landscape; reflects the mysterious instability and vibrating life of the forms within.

ORIGINS: Expressionism, Dada, Surrealism.

GORKY: *Composition.* 1932-33. Oil, 36 x 48″. Collection Mr. and Mrs. Donald Grossman

OPPOSITE: GORKY: *Agony.* 1947. Oil, 40 x 50½″. The Museum of Modern Art, A. Conger Goodyear Fund

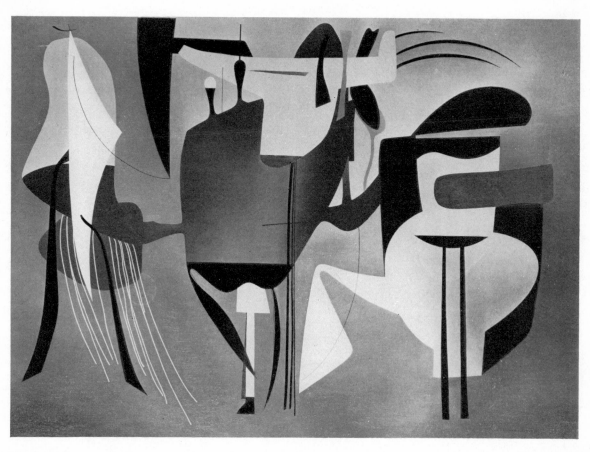

HOWARD: *Trinity*. 1941. Oil, 24 x 34″. The Art Institute of Chicago

CARLES: *Composition III.* 1931-32. Oil, $51\frac{3}{8}$ x $38\frac{3}{4}''$. The Museum of Modern Art, gift of Leopold Stokowski

LASSAW: *Composition in Steel*. 1938. Hammered steel, 18½″ high. Owned by the artist

DE KOONING: *Painting*. 1948. Ripolin enamel and oil, 42⅝ x 56⅛″. The Museum of Modern Art, Purchase Fund

DE KOONING: *Excavation*. 1950. Oil, 6′ 7″ x 8′ 4″. Egan Gallery

ROTHKO: *No. 14*. 1949. Oil, 66 x 41¼". Betty Parsons Gallery

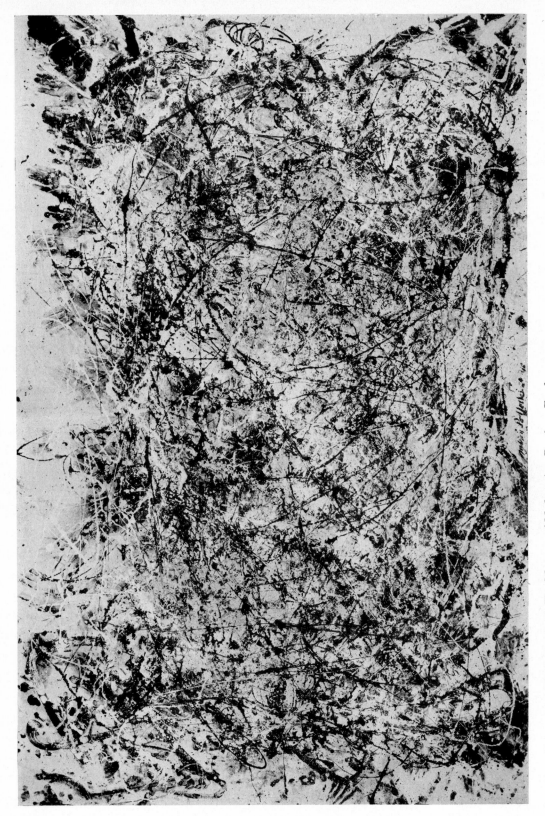

POLLOCK: *No. 1.* 1948. Oil, 5' 8" x 8' 8". The Museum of Modern Art, Purchase Fund

SELIGER: *Winterscape*. 1948-49. Tempera, 13⅝ x 11⅜″. Willard Gallery

KAMROWSKI: *The Urgent Hour.* 1949.
Oil, 35¾ x 48¼″. Collection Brooks Jackson

POUSETTE-DART: *No. 11: A Presence.* 1949.
Oil, 25⅛ x 21⅛″. The Museum of
Modern Art, Katharine Cornell Fund

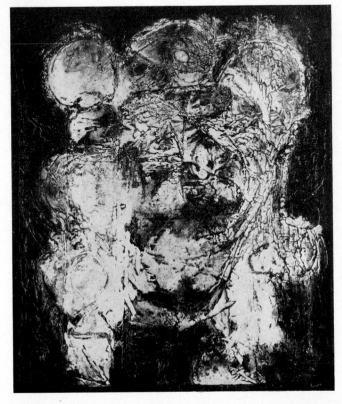

BROOKS: *No. 27.* 1950. Oil, 37⅛ x 46″. Peridot Gallery

DAY: *Prima Materia*. 1948.
Oil, 38½ x 30¾". Bertha Schaefer Gallery

GERTRUDE GREENE: *Monumentality*. 1949.
Oil, 48 x 36". Laurel Gallery

STAMOS: *Sacrifice of Chronos, No. 2.* 1948. Oil, 48 x 36". The Phillips Gallery

BAZIOTES: *Blue Mirror*. 1948. Oil, 24 x 30″. Collection Dr. F. W. Cooper, Jr.

REYNAL: *Singular Sun*. 1950.
Mosaic, 22¾ x 38½".
Collection William Alexander,
courtesy of the Hugo Gallery

NOGUCHI: *The Gunas.* 1948.
Tennessee marble, 6′ 1¼″ high.
Egan Gallery

LIPTON: *Invocation*. 1950. Lead and iron, 7′ 7″ high.
Betty Parsons Gallery

GRIPPE: *Symbolic Figure No. 4.* 1946. Bronze, 17″ high. Willard Gallery

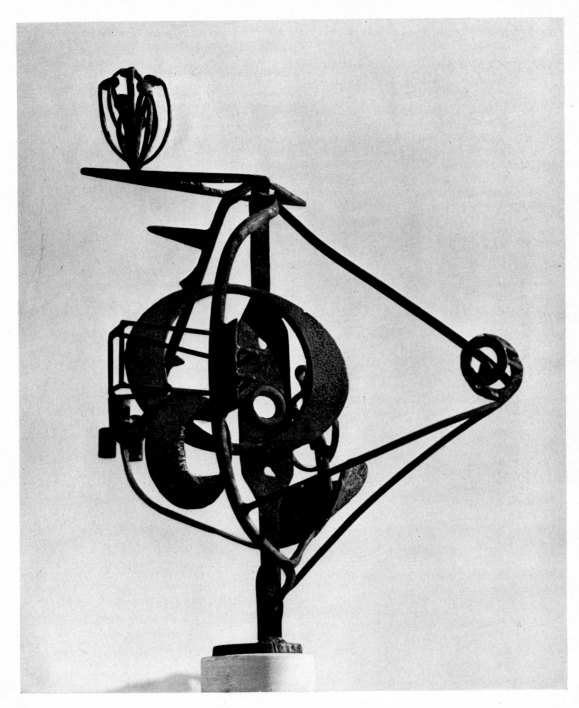

Smith: *Blackburn: Song of an Irish Blacksmith.* 1949–50. Iron, 46½″ high. Willard Gallery

CATALOGUE OF THE EXHIBITION

LENDERS

Charles Alan, New York; William Alexander, New York; Mr. and Mrs. Walter C. Arensberg, Hollywood; Dr. F. W. Cooper, Jr., Emory University; John Ferren, New York; Lyonel Feininger, New York; Mr. and Mrs. Donald Grossman, New York; Mrs. Edith Gregor Halpert, New York; Brooks Jackson, New York; Ibram Lassaw, New York; Wright Ludington, Santa Barbara; Mr. and Mrs. Roy R. Neuberger, New York; Miss Georgia O'Keeffe, Abiquiu, New Mexico; Walter Pach, New York; Mrs. William A. Pedlar, New York; Man Ray, Hollywood; Morgan Russell, Broomall, Pa.; Mr. and Mrs. Hudson Walker, New York; Max Weber, Great Neck, L.I.

The American Academy of Arts and Letters, New York; The Art Institute of Chicago; State University of Iowa, Iowa City; The Metropolitan Museum of Art, New York;

The Miller Company Collection "Painting Towards Architecture," Meriden, Conn.; University Gallery, University of Minnesota, Minneapolis; The Newark Museum; The Phillips Gallery, Washington, D.C.; Yale University Art Gallery, *Société Anonyme* Collection, New Haven.

Earl Stendahl Gallery, Hollywood; and Artists' Gallery; Buchholz Gallery; The Downtown Gallery; Egan Gallery; Grand Central Moderns Gallery; Hugo Gallery; Sidney Janis Gallery; Kootz Gallery; Kraushaar Galleries; Laurel Gallery; Mortimer Levitt Gallery; Pierre Matisse Gallery; J. B. Neumann Gallery; Betty Parsons Gallery; Passedoit Gallery, Peridot Gallery; Pinacotheca Gallery; A. P. Rosenberg & Co., Inc.; Bertha Schaefer Gallery; Catherine Viviano Gallery; Maynard Walker Gallery; Willard Gallery; all of New York.

CATALOGUE

Dates of exhibition: January 23 to March 25, 1951. In dimensions height precedes width unless otherwise indicated.

ALBERS, JOSEPH

Born Westphalia, Germany, 1888. Studied Berlin, Essen and Munich. 1923-33, taught at Bauhaus until closing of school by German government. To U.S. 1933. Headed art department, Black Mountain College, 1933-50. Now directs Department of Design, Yale University. Has painted in abstract style since 1920. Lives in New Haven, Conn.

  1 *Dark*. 1947. Oil, 26½ x 38″. Lent by the Sidney Janis Gallery, New York. *Ill. p. 76*

BAZIOTES, WILLIAM

Born Pittsburgh, Pa., 1912. Studied National Academy of Design. Began working in abstract style about 1941. First one-man exhibition Art of This Century, New York, 1944. Lives in New York.

  2 *Blue Mirror*. 1948. Oil, 24 x 30″. Lent by Dr. F. W. Cooper, Jr., Emory University, Georgia. *Ill. in color, p. 141*

BROOKS, JAMES

Born St. Louis, 1906. Studied Southern Methodist University and Art Students League. First one-man show, Peridot Gallery, 1950. Lives in New York.

  3 *No. 27*. 1950. Oil, 37⅛ x 46″. Lent by the Peridot Gallery, New York. *Ill. p. 133*

BROWNE, BYRON

Born Yonkers, N.Y., 1907. Studied National Academy of Design, 1924-28. First one-man show, New School for Social Research, 1936. Exhibited with American Abstract Artists, 1937-46. Lives in New York.

  4 *Variations on a Still Life*. 1938. Oil, 47 x 36″. Lent by the Grand Central Moderns Gallery, New York. *Ill. p. 107*

BRUCE, PATRICK HENRY

Born Virginia, 1880. Studied with Robert Henri. Settled permanently in Paris, 1907. With other American painters, Max Weber, A. B. Frost, Jr., studied under Henri Matisse, 1907. Later, with Frost joined Orphist movement of Robert Delaunay. Exhibited pure abstractions with Delaunay and others in *Salon des Indépendants*, Paris, 1914. Exhibited New York: Armory Show, 1913; Society of Independent Artists, 1917; Montross Gallery, 1917, 1918; *Société Anonyme*, 1920. Died Paris, 1937.

  5 *Composition II*. Before 1918. Oil, 38¼ x 51″. Lent by the Yale University Art Gallery, New Haven, *Société Anonyme* Collection. *Ill. p. 53*

CALDER, ALEXANDER

Born Philadelphia, 1898. Graduated in engineering Stevens Institute, 1919. Worked several years as engineer. Studied Art Students League, c. 1923-26. Wire sculpture, 1926-27. First trip to Paris in 1926, returned annually until 1934. Interest in abstract art aroused by Mondrian's studio. Exhibited first abstract constructions Paris, 1931; joined van Doesburg's *Abstraction-Creation* group, Paris. Devised first wind-propelled constructions (mobiles), 1932. Since 1930 has worked consistently in abstract style. Lives in Roxbury, Conn.

6 *Feathers*. 1931. Wood, steel rod, lead, 39½" high. Lent by the Buchholz Gallery, New York. *Ill. p. 108*

7 *Spiny*. 1942. Sheet aluminum painted, 26" high. Lent by the Buchholz Gallery, New York. *Ill. p. 109*

8 *Gypsophila II*. 1950. Metal and wire, painted, 54" high, 65" wide. Lent by the Buchholz Gallery, New York. *Ill. p. 111*

CALLAHAN, KENNETH

Born Spokane, Washington, 1906. Studied University of Washington. Traveled 1926-28: London, Paris, Florence, Mexico. First New York one-man show, American British Art Center, 1946. Lives in Seattle.

9 *Abstraction I*. 1950. Tempera, 20 x 24¼". Lent by Maynard Walker Gallery, New York, *Ill. p. 98*

CARLES, ARTHUR B.

Born Philadelphia, 1882. Studied Pennsylvania Academy of Arts. Paris, 1905 and 1907-12, 1920 and 1929. Exhibited Armory Show, 1913. Taught at Pennsylvania Academy of Arts, 1917-25. Near-abstract and abstract compositions in '30s. Lives in Chestnut Hill, Pa.

10 *Composition III*. 1931-32. Oil, 51⅜ x 38¾". The Museum of Modern Art, New York, gift of Leopold Stokowski. *Ill. p. 130*

CAVALLON, GIORGIO

Born Italy, 1904. Studied National Academy of Design, Tiffany Foundation, and with Charles Hawthorne and Hans Hofmann. Has exhibited with American Abstract Artists since 1936. Lives in New York.

11 *Abstraction*. 1950. Oil, 36 x 42". Lent by the Egan Gallery, New York. *Ill. p. 75*

COGGESHALL, CALVERT

Born near Utica, N.Y., 1907. Studied fine arts and architecture at University of Pennsylvania, c. 1925-28 and Art Students League. Europe 1937-38. Has worked as architectural and furniture designer. Lives in North Stonington, Conn.

12 *Nightscape*. 1950. Oil, 27 x 48". Lent by the Betty Parsons Gallery, New York. *Ill. p. 99*

CONOVER, ROBERT

Born Philadelphia, 1920. Studied Philadelphia Museum School, Art Students League and Brooklyn Museum School. First one-man show, Laurel Gallery, 1950. Lives in New York.

13 *Gray Abstraction*. 1949. Oil, 51 x 30". Lent by the Laurel Gallery, New York. *Ill. p. 119*

COVERT, JOHN

Born Pittsburgh, Pa., 1882. Munich 1908-12, studied on scholarship from German government. Paris 1912-14, traveled England and Continent. Exhibited Paris Salon, 1914. Exhibited with Society of Independent Artists, New York, 1917. Developed highly individual abstract style, 1915-23. Did not paint between 1923 and 1949. Lives in Pittsburgh.

14 *Temptation of St. Anthony*. 1916. Oil, 25¾ x 23¾". Lent by the Yale University Art Gallery, New Haven, *Société Anonyme* Collection. *Ill. p. 48*

15 *Brass Band*. 1919. Oil and string on board, 26 x 24". Lent by the Yale University Art Gallery, New Haven, *Société Anonyme* Collection. *Ill. p. 49*

CRAWFORD, RALSTON

Born St. Catharines, Ontario, Canada, 1906. Studied Otis Art Institute, Los Angeles; Pennsylvania Academy; Barnes Foundation and in Europe. First one-man show Boyer Gallery, Philadelphia, 1937. Lives in New York.

16 *From the Bridge*. 1942. Oil, 28 x 40¼". Lent by The Downtown Gallery, New York. *Ill. p. 91*

DAVIS, STUART

Born Philadelphia, 1894. 1910-13: studied with Henri; worked as cartoonist and illustrator. Exhibited Armory Show, 1913; particularly impressed by van Gogh and Gauguin. First one-man show, 1917. Painted "collages" suggested by Cubism, 1921. Abstract still life compositions, 1927-28. Paris 1928-29. Style increasingly abstract since 1938. Lives in New York.

17 *Lucky Strike*. 1921. Oil, 33⅛ x 18". Lent by The Downtown Gallery, New York. *Ill. p. 62*

18 *Salt Shaker*. 1931. Oil, 49⅞ x 32". Lent by Mrs. Edith Gregor Halpert, New York. *Ill. p. 104*

19 *For Internal Use Only*. 1945. Oil, 45 x 28". Lent by the Miller Company Collection "Painting Towards Architecture," Meriden, Conn. *Ill. in color, p. 105*

149

DAY, WORDEN

Born Columbus, Ohio, 1916. Studied Art Students League. Lives in Laramie, Wyoming.

20 *Prima Materia*. 1948. Oil, 38½ x 30¾". Lent by the Bertha Schaefer Gallery, New York, *Ill. p. 139*

DILLER, BURGOYNE

Born New York, 1906. Studied Michigan State College, Art Students League, and with H. Hofmann. Since 1934 has worked in the *Stijl* tradition of van Doesburg and Mondrian. Lives in New York.

21 *Composition*. 1943-44. Oil, 42 x 42". Lent by the Pinacotheca Gallery, New York. *Ill. p. 72*

DOVE, ARTHUR G.

Born Canandaigua, N.Y., 1880. Began art training at age of nine, Geneva, N.Y. Worked as illustrator, c. 1904-08. France and Italy, c. 1908-10. First exhibited 1910, Stieglitz gallery "291." Participated Forum Exhibition, 1916. Abstractions from nature begun c. 1912. Died Huntington, N.Y., 1946.

22 *Goin' Fishin'*. c. 1925. Collage, 19½ x 24". Lent by The Phillips Gallery, Washington, D.C. *Ill. p. 63*

23 *Sand Barge*. 1930. Oil, 30 x 40". Lent by The Phillips Gallery, Washington, D.C. *Ill. p. 93*

24 *Rising Tide*. 1944. Oil, 27 x 36". Lent by The Downtown Gallery, New York. *Ill. p. 94*

DREIER, KATHERINE S.

Born 1877, Brooklyn, N.Y. Studied with Walter Shirlaw and in Munich, Florence, Paris. Exhibited in Armory Show, 1913. With Marcel Duchamp and Man Ray founded *Société Anonyme*, Museum of Modern Art, 1920 which promoted advanced American and European work by exhibition, publication and purchase. Lives in Milford, Conn.

25 *Abstract Portrait of Marcel Duchamp*. 1918. Oil, 18 x 32". The Museum of Modern Art, New York, Mrs. John D. Rockefeller, Jr., Purchase Fund. *Ill. p. 59*

ERNST, JIMMY

Born 1920, near Cologne, Germany. Came to U.S., 1938; began painting 1940. Self-taught. First one-man show Norlyst Gallery, 1934. Lives in New York.

26 *A Time for Fear*. 1949. Oil, 23⅞ x 20". The Museum of Modern Art, New York, Katharine Cornell Fund. *Ill. p. 121*

FEININGER, LYONEL

Born New York, 1871. To Germany in 1887 where he lived until 1937. Studied Hamburg; Berlin. Illustrator for German, French and American journals, 1894-1906. Three sojourns in Paris: 1892-93, 1906-08, 1911. First cubist painting, 1912. Has worked consistently ever since in modified cubist style. Taught at Bauhaus, 1919-25. Exhibited extensively Germany, 1920-33. In U.S. first exhibited, 1923, Anderson Gallery. Settled permanently U.S., 1937. Lives in New York.

27 *Zirchow VII*. 1918. Oil, 31½ x 39½". Lent by the artist. *Ill. p. 45*

28 *Bridge V*. 1919. Oil, 31¾ x 39⅝". Lent by the Buchholz Gallery, New York. *Ill. p. 45*

29 *Vita Nova*. 1947. Oil, 31½ x 39½". Lent by the Buchholz Gallery, New York. *Ill. p. 97*

FERBER, HERBERT

Born New York, 1906. Studied City College, Columbia University (dentistry and oral surgery); Beaux-Arts Institute of Design and Tiffany Foundation. First one-man sculpture exhibition, Midtown Galleries, 1937. Began working in abstract style c. 1942. Lives in New York.

30 *The Bow*. 1950. Lead, 48" high. Lent by the Betty Parsons Gallery, New York, *Ill. p. 124*

FERREN, JOHN

Born 1905, near Pendleton, Oregon. First worked as sculptor. Europe, 1929-38: turned from sculpture to painting, c. 1931. Studied engraving, Paris, S. W. Hayter's Studio 17. Made series of engravings printed on plaster, 1936-37. Returned U.S., 1938. Lives in New York.

31 *Composition on Green*. 1936. Oil, 28¾ x 39". Lent by the artist. *Ill. p. 71*

32 *Painting*. 1950. Oil, 22 x 30". Lent by the artist. *Ill. p. 117*

FULLER, SUE

Born Pittsburgh, 1914. Studied Carnegie Institute of Technology and Teachers' College and with Arthur Young and S. W. Hayter. Abstract compositions in string begun about 1947. Lives in New York.

33 *String Construction in Yellow and Grey*. 1946. String, 30 x 24". Lent by the Bertha Schaefer Gallery, New York. *Ill. p. 84*

GALLATIN, A. E.

Born 1882, Villanova, Pa. Studied New York Law School. Self-taught as painter. In 1927 opened to public large collection of abstract European and American art (Gallery of Living Art, New York University). Since 1937 has exhibited annually with American Abstract Artists. Lives in New York.

34 *Forms*. 1949-50. Oil, 30 x 23". Lent by the Pinacotheca Gallery, New York. *Ill. p. 80*

GLARNER, FRITZ

Born Zurich, Switzerland, 1899. Lived Italy c. 1914-22. Studied Royal Institute of Fine Arts, Naples. Paris c. 1922-36. Settled permanently U.S., 1936. First one-man show in U.S., Kootz Gallery, 1946. Works in tradition of Mondrian. Lives in New York.

35 *Relational Painting.* 1947-48. Oil, 43⅛ x 42¼". The Museum of Modern Art, New York, Purchase Fund. *Ill. in color, p. 73*

GOLUBOV, MAURICE

Born Vetka, Russia, 1905. To U.S. 1917. Studied National Academy of Design, 1920-23. First one-man show, Artists' Gallery, 1941. Has exhibited with American Abstract Artists since 1945. Lives in New York.

36 *Fantasy.* 1945. Oil, 30 x 46". Lent by the Artists' Gallery, New York. *Ill. p. 116*

GORKY, ARSHILE

Born Hayotz Dzore, Armenia, 1904. Painted from childhood. Studied Polytechnic Institute, Tiflis 1916-18. To U.S. 1920. Studied engineering Brown University; painted in free time. To New York 1925. Entered and was dismissed from three American art schools: Providence, 1920; Boston, 1924; New York, 1925. Began working in partially abstract style c. 1929 under influence of Picasso. Free-form organic abstractions from c. 1936-37. Died by suicide, Connecticut, 1948.

37 *Composition.* 1932-33. Oil, 36 x 48". Lent by Mr. and Mrs. Donald Grossman, New York. *Ill. p. 126*

38 *Agony.* 1947. Oil, 40 x 50½". The Museum of Modern Art, New York, A. Conger Goodyear Fund. *Ill. in color, p. 127*

GREENE, BALCOMB

Born 1904, Niagara Falls, N.Y. Studied Syracuse University, Columbia University, New York University, and Paris and Vienna. Self-taught as painter. Exhibited with American Abstract Artists, 1937-45. Lives in Pittsburgh.

39 *Blue Space.* 1941. Oil, 20 x 30". Lent by the Bertha Schaefer Gallery, New York. *Ill. p. 86*

GREENE, GERTRUDE

Born New York, 1911. Studied Da Vinci Art School, New York. Exhibited with American Abstract Artists, 1937-44. Lives in Pittsburgh.

40 *Monumentality.* 1949. Oil, 48 x 36". Lent by the Laurel Gallery, New York. *Ill. p. 139*

GRIPPE, PETER

Born Buffalo, N.Y., 1912. Formal training begun at eleven, Albright Art School, Buffalo. To New York 1939. First one-man show, Orrefors Galleries, 1942. Lives in New York.

41 *Symbolic Figure No. 4.* 1946. Bronze, 17" high. Lent by the Willard Gallery, New York. *Ill. p. 146*

GUSTON, PHILIP

Born Montreal, 1913. Studied Otis Art Institute, Los Angeles, 1930. First one-man show, Midtown Galleries, 1945. Began working in abstract style c. 1948. Lives in New York.

42 *Painting.* 1950. Oil, 34 x 62". Lent by the Peridot Gallery, New York.

HARTLEY, MARSDEN

Born Lewiston, Maine, 1877. Studied at Chase School and National Academy of Design, New York, 1898-1900. Europe 1912-13: Paris, experimented briefly with Cubism; later abstract work encouraged by Delaunay. Exhibited Munich with Blue Rider group, and in First Autumn Salon, Berlin, 1913, at invitation of Franz Marc. Returned to U.S. 1913; exhibited in Armory Show. Europe 1914-16; continued abstract painting in Germany. One-man show, Berlin. Returned to U.S. 1916; participated in Forum Exhibition. Exhibited with Society of Independent Artists, New York, 1917. After 1918 returned to traditional subject-matter increasingly expressionistic in style. Died Ellsworth, Maine, 1943.

43 *"E."* 1915. Oil, 47½ x 47½". Lent by the estate of the artist, courtesy of A. P. Rosenberg & Co., Inc., New York. *Ill. in color, p. 51*

44 *Abstraction.* c. 1916. Oil, 13¼ x 16¼". Lent by Mr. and Mrs. Hudson Walker, courtesy of the University Gallery, University of Minnesota, Minneapolis. *Ill. p. 55*

HELIKER, JOHN

Born Yonkers, N.Y., 1909. Studied Art Students League. First one-man show, Hudson Walker Gallery, 1941. Europe 1948-49 and 1950. Lives in New York.

45 *Scava.* 1950. Oil, 11½ x 18". Lent by The American Academy of Arts and Letters, New York. Childe Hassam Purchase Fund. *Ill. p. 101*

HOFMANN, HANS

Born 1880, Weissenberg, Germany. Studied in Munich. Paris 1904-14. Conducted own school, Munich, 1915-32. Settled permanently in U.S., 1932. Opened school in New York, 1934. Work increasingly abstract since 1939. Lives in New York.

46 *The Window.* 1950. Oil, 48 x 35¾". Lent by the Metropolitan Museum of Art, New York, gift of Mr. and Mrs. Roy R. Neuberger. *Ill. p. 120*

HOLTY, CARL

Born Freiburg, Germany, 1900; to U.S. same year. Studied Art Institute of Chicago, National Academy of Design, and in Munich with Hans Hofmann. Europe 1925-33. First one-man show New York, Nierendorf Gallery, 1938. Exhibited with American Abstract Artists, 1937-46. Lives in New York.

47 *Equestrian.* 1942. Oil, 54 x 36″. Lent by the Kootz Gallery, New York. *Ill. p. 78*

HOWARD, CHARLES

Born Montclair, N.J., 1899. Began painting in 1924 after two years in Europe. Journeyman painter in decorating studio, 1926-31. First one-man show, Julien Levy Gallery, New York, 1933. England 1933-40: associated with English surrealist group, 1936-38. San Francisco 1940-46. Lives in England.

48 *Trinity.* 1941. Oil, 24 x 34″. Lent by The Art Institute of Chicago. *Ill. p. 129*

KAMROWSKI, GEROME

Born Warren, Minnesota, 1914. Studied St. Paul School of Art and Art Students League. Lives in Ann Arbor, Michigan.

49 *The Urgent Hour.* 1949. Oil, 35¾ x 48¼″. Lent by Brooks Jackson, New York. *Ill. p. 137*

KENT, ADALINE

Born Kentfield, California, 1900. Studied Vassar College, California School of Fine Arts, and in Paris with Bourdelle. Began working in abstract style c. 1946. Lives in San Francisco.

50 *Presence.* 1948. Magnesite, 43¾″ high. Lent by the Betty Parsons Gallery, New York. *Ill. p. 122*

KIENBUSCH, WILLIAM

Born New York, 1914. Studied Princeton University; Colorado Springs Fine Arts Center with H. V. Poore; in Paris, at Colarossi and with A. Rattner; New York with A. Refregier and Stuart Davis. First one-man show, Kraushaar Galleries, 1949. Lives in New York.

51 *Low Tide.* 1950. Gouache, 22½ x 31″. Lent by the Kraushaar Galleries, New York. *Ill. p. 99*

KNATHS, KARL

Born Eau Claire, Wisconsin, 1891. 1911-17, studied at Art Institute of Chicago. Impressed by Chicago Armory Show 1913, but continued painting under impressionist influence for several years. Settled in Provincetown, c. 1920. First exhibited Daniel Gallery, 1924. Work approached pure

abstraction about 1930, stimulated by theoretical writings of Klee. Lives in Provincetown.

52 *Maritime. 1931.* Oil, 40 x 32″. Lent by The Phillips Gallery, Washington, D.C. *Ill. p. 103*

de KOONING, WILLEM

Born Rotterdam, Holland, 1904. Left school at twelve to work as apprentice in painting and decorating firm. Studied evenings at Rotterdam Academy of Fine Arts; introduced to *de Stijl* principles c. 1920 by one of teachers, Jongert. To U.S. 1926; worked for a time as housepainter. Began painting in abstract style c. 1934. First one-man show Egan Gallery, New York, 1948. Lives in New York.

53 *Painting.* 1948. Ripolin enamel and oil, 42⅝ x 56⅛″. The Museum of Modern Art, New York, Purchase Fund. *Ill. p. 132*

54 *Excavation.* 1950. Oil, 6′ 7″ x 8′ 4″. Lent by the Egan Gallery, New York. *Ill. p. 133*

LASSAW, IBRAM

Born Alexandria, Egypt, 1913. Studied Clay Club, Beaux-Arts Institute of Design. Has exhibited with American Abstract Artists since 1937. Lives in New York.

55 *Composition in Steel.* 1938. Hammered steel, 18½″ high. Lent by the artist. *Ill. p. 131*

56 *The Milky Way: A Polymorphic Space.* 1950. Plastic metal, 51½″ high. Lent by the artist. *Ill. p. 123*

LEWANDOWSKI, EDMUND D.

Born Milwaukee, Wisconsin, 1914. Studied Layton School of Art, Milwaukee. Lives in Tallahassee, Florida.

57 *Christmas Tree.* 1950. Oil, 40 x 22″. Lent by The Downtown Gallery, New York. *Ill. p. 89*

LEWIS, NORMAN

Born New York, 1909. Studied briefly Columbia University. Began painting 1944 in studio of sculptor, Augusta Savage. Lives in New York.

58 *Urban.* 1950. Oil, 50 x 29¾″. Lent by the Willard Gallery, New York. *Ill. p. 100*

LIPPOLD, RICHARD

Born 1915, Milwaukee, Wisconsin. Studied University of Chicago and Art Institute of Chicago (industrial design), 1933-37. Industrial designer, 1937-41. Began working as sculptor, 1942. Self-taught. First one-man show, Willard Gallery, 1947. Lives in New York.

59 *Primordial Figure.* 1947. Copper and brass, 8′ 1″ high. Lent by Mrs. William A. Pedlar, New York. *Ill. p. 82*

LIPTON, SEYMOUR

Born New York, 1903. Studied College of City of New York, Columbia University (dentistry). First one-man show, A.C.A. Gallery, 1938. Has worked in abstract style since 1944. Lives in New York.

60 *Invocation.* 1950. Lead and iron, 7′ 7″ high. Lent by the Betty Parsons Gallery, New York. *Ill. p. 145*

MACDONALD-WRIGHT, STANTON

Born Charlottesville, Va., 1890. Family name Van Kranken. To France 1907. Studied Paris, *Ecole des Beaux-Arts, Académie Julien* and the Sorbonne. About 1912 formulated Synchromism in Paris with Morgan Russell. Exhibited 1913: New York (Carroll Gallery and Armory Show), Munich, Paris (Bernheim-Jeune Galleries and *Salon des Indépendants*). Returned to U.S. 1916. One-man show, Stieglitz gallery "291," 1917. Participated in first New York Independents show, 1917. Returned to figurative painting, c. 1919-20. Lives in Santa Monica, California.

61 *Conception Synchromy.* 1916. Oil, 66 x 24″. Lent by the Earl Stendhal Gallery, Hollywood. *Ill. p. 54*

62 *Synchromy.* 1917. Oil, 31 x 24″. The Museum of Modern Art, New York, given anonymously. *Ill. p. 55*

MARIN, JOHN

Born Rutherford, N. J., 1870. Worked first as architect. Studied painting at Pennsylvania Academy of Fine Arts and Art Students League, 1899-1903. Paris 1905-09 and 1910-11. First one-man show, 1910, Stieglitz gallery "291." Exhibited in Armory Show, 1913, and Forum Exhibition, 1916. Explosive compositions c. 1912-16 owe something to Cubism or Futurism. Style otherwise independent of international abstract traditions. Lives in Cliffside, N.J.

63 *Tree Forms.* 1915. Watercolor, 14⅛ x 16⅜″. Lent by Charles Alan, New York. *Ill. p. 46*

64 *Lower Manhattan (Composing Derived from Top of Woolworth).* 1922. Watercolor, 21⅝ x 26⅞″. The Museum of Modern Art, New York, acquired through the Lillie P. Bliss Bequest. *Ill. p. 47*

65 *The Fog Lifts.* 1949. Oil, 22 x 28″. Lent by The Downtown Gallery, New York. *Ill. p. 96*

McNEIL, GEORGE

Born New York, 1909. Studied Art Students League, Pratt Institute and with Hans Hofmann. Has exhibited with American Abstract Artists since 1937. Lives in New York.

66 *Abstraction.* 1949. Oil, 30 x 24″. Lent by the Egan Gallery, New York. *Ill. p. 117*

MODEL, EVSA

Born Russian Siberia, 1900. Lived in Far East, India, Egypt and Paris. To U.S. 1938. Lives in New York.

67 *Uptown.* 1947. Oil, 62 x 47″. Lent by the Sidney Janis Gallery, New York. *Ill. p. 90*

MORGAN, RANDALL

Born 1920, Kingstown, Indiana. Studied University of Indiana, Cincinnati University and Columbia University. Lives in New York. Now in Italy.

68 *Mediterranean Night.* 1949. Oil, 10⅜ x 15½″. Lent by the J. B. Neumann Gallery, New York. *Ill. p. 101*

69 *Cliff City.* 1950. Oil, 9⅞ x 15½″. Lent by the J. B. Neumann Gallery, New York.

MORRIS, GEORGE L. K.

Born New York, 1905. Studied Yale University, 1928; Art Students League, 1929-30; and with Léger, Paris, 1930. First one-man show, Valentine Gallery, New York, 1933. Exhibited with American Abstract Artists from 1937. Lives in New York.

70 *Concretion.* 1936. Oil, 54¾ x 70½″. Lent by The Downtown Gallery, New York. *Ill. p. 70*

71 *Suspended Discs.* 1950. Oil, 23 x 19″. Lent by The Downtown Gallery, New York. *Ill. p. 79*

MOTHERWELL, ROBERT

Born Aberdeen, Washington, 1915. Studied Stanford University, 1933-37; philosophy, Harvard, 1937-38; architecture, Columbia, 1940-41. Self-taught as painter; studied etching and engraving with Kurt Seligmann and S. W. Hayter. Has traveled in British Columbia, Mexico. Europe 1935 and 1938-39. First one-man show, Art of This Century, 1944. Lives in New York.

72 *Western Air.* 1946-47. Oil, 72 x 54″. The Museum of Modern Art, New York, Purchase Fund (by exchange). *Ill. p. 114*

NOGUCHI, ISAMU

Born Los Angeles, 1904. Childhood Japan. Returned to U.S. 1918. Worked briefly with Gutzon Borglum, 1922. After two years pre-medical studies devoted full time to sculpture. Paris, 1927-28, worked as assistant to Brancusi. Returned to U.S. 1929, exhibited abstract metal constructions at Eugene Schoen Gallery, New York. Japan and China 1930-31: studied drawing in Peking, worked with potter in Kyoto. Traveled Mediterranean, India, Indonesia, Indo-China and Japan, 1949-50. Has also worked in industrial and theatre design. Lives in New York.

73 *The Gunas.* 1948. Tennessee marble, 6′ 1¼″ high. Lent by the Egan Gallery, New York. *Ill. p. 144*

O'KEEFFE, GEORGIA

Born Sun Prairie, Wisconsin, 1887. Studied 1904-08, Art Institute of Chicago and Art Students League, N.Y. under Chase. Taught in Texas, 1912-18; studied summers with Bement and A. W. Dow, 1914-16. Abstract drawings 1915. First one-man show, 1917, Stieglitz gallery "291." Lives in Abiquiu, New Mexico.

74 From the *Pelvis Series*. 1947. Oil, 39¾ x 48″. Lent by the artist. *Ill. p. 95*

PACH, WALTER

Born New York, 1883. Studied with Chase and Henri. Paris 1904, 1905, 1907-8 and 1910-13. With Arthur B. Davies and Walt Kuhn selected and organized the International Exhibition of Modern Art (Armory Show), New York, 1913. Exhibited with Society of Independent Artists, New York, 1917-19. Lives in New York.

75 *St. Patrick's at Night*. 1916. Oil, 18 x 24″. Lent by the artist. *Ill. p. 48*

PEREIRA, I. RICE

Born Boston, 1907. To New York about 1914. Studied Art Students League, 1928-31, and in Paris and Italy, 1931-32. First one-man show, A.C.A. Gallery, New York, 1933. Lives in New York.

76 *Composition in White*. 1942. Mixed medium on parchment, 18 x 18″. Lent by The Newark Museum. *Ill. p. 77*

POLLOCK, JACKSON

Born Cody, Wyoming, 1912. Studied at Art Students League with Thomas Benton, 1929-31. Made twelve sketching trips across the country. Began working in abstract style about 1940. First one-man show at Art of This Century, 1944. Lives in East Hampton, Long Island.

77 *No. 1*. 1948. Oil, 5′ 8″ x 8′ 8″. The Museum of Modern Art, New York, Purchase Fund. *Ill. p. 135*

POUSETTE-DART, RICHARD

Born St. Paul, Minnesota, 1916. Self-taught. First one-man show, Artists' Gallery, 1941. Lives in Sloatsburg, N.Y.

78 *No. 11: A Presence*. 1949. Oil, 25⅛ x 21⅛″. The Museum of Modern Art, New York, Katharine Cornell Fund. *Ill. p. 137*

RAY, MAN

Born Philadelphia, 1890. Gave up study of architecture and engineering in 1907 to study painting, National Academy. First one-man exhibition, 1912. After Armory Show, 1913-17, work increasingly abstract. Participated in Forum Exhibition, 1916. Formed New York Dada group with Du-

champ and Picabia. Associated with Katherine S. Dreier and Marcel Duchamp in *Société Anonyme*, 1920. Paris, 1921-40; participated in Paris dada and surrealist movements. Has worked extensively in photography; developed rayograph technique; has made four abstract or surrealist films. Returned to U.S. 1940. Lives in Hollywood.

79 *Black Widow*. 1915. Oil, 70 x 34″. Lent by the artist. *Ill. p. 56*

80 *The Rope Dancer Accompanies Herself with Her Shadows*. 1916. Oil, 52 x 73⅜″. Lent by the State University of Iowa, Iowa City. *Ill. p. 57*

81 *Aerograph*. 1919. Airbrush and watercolor, 27 x 20″. Lent by the artist. *Ill. p. 58*

REINHARDT, AD

Born Buffalo, N.Y., 1913. Studied Columbia University, New York University. Self-taught as painter. Exhibited with American Abstract Artists, 1939-46. First one-man exhibition, Artists' Gallery, New York, 1944. Lives in New York.

82 *No. 11*. 1949. Oil, 50 x 20″. Lent by the Betty Parsons Gallery, New York. *Ill. p. 113*

REYNAL, JEANNE

Born New York, 1903. Worked in Paris as apprentice to mosaic-maker, Boris Anrep, 1930-39. Lives in New York.

83 *Singular Sun*. 1950. Mosaic, 22¾ x 38½″. Lent by William Alexander, through the courtesy of the Hugo Gallery, New York. *Ill. p. 143*

de RIVERA, JOSÉ

Born New Orleans, 1904. Studied drawing with John W. Norton in Chicago. Self-taught as sculptor. Traveled Spain, France, Italy, Sicily, North Africa. First one-man show Levitt Gallery, 1947. Began working in abstract style c. 1940. Lives in New York.

84 *Yellow Black*. 1946-47. Aluminum, 60″ long. Lent by the Mortimer Levitt Gallery, New York. *Ill. p. 81*

ROSZAK, THEODORE J.

Born Posen, Poland, 1907. Studied Columbia University, National Academy of Design, Art Institute of Chicago. Europe 1929-31. First one-man show (paintings and prints), Allerton Gallery, Chicago, 1928. First abstract constructions, c. 1935. Lives in New York.

85 *Construction in White*. 1940. Painted wood and plastic, 36 x 36″. Lent by the Pierre Matisse Gallery, New York. *Ill. p. 83*

86 *Spatial Construction*. 1943. Steel wire and wood, painted, 23¼″ high. Lent by the Pierre Matisse Gallery, New York. *Ill. p. 83*

ROTHKO, MARK

Born 1903, Dwinsk, Russia. To U.S. (Portland, Ore.) 1913. Yale University 1921-23. Studied with Max Weber, 1926; style expressionist until 1939. First abstract painting exhibited at Art of This Century, 1945. Lives in New York.

87 *No. 14.* 1949. Oil, 66 x 41¼". Lent by the Betty Parsons Gallery, New York. *Ill. p. 134*

RUSSELL, ALFRED

Born Chicago, 1920. Studied painting at Art Students League, 1940; history of art, Columbia University, 1946. First one-man show, Weyhe Gallery, 1946. Lives in New York.

88 *Rue Saint Denis.* 1948-50. Oil, 54 x 40". Lent by the Peridot Gallery, New York. *Ill. p. 118*

RUSSELL, MORGAN

Born New York, 1886. Studied with Robert Henri. To France 1906. With S. Macdonald-Wright formulated Synchromism about 1912. First synchromist canvases exhibited at *Salon des Indépendants*, spring, 1913. One-man show with Macdonald-Wright, Munich, June, 1913, and November at Bernheim-Jeune Galleries, Paris. Paris show included first abstract synchromist picture. Included in Armory Show, New York, 1913. After 1919 returned to figurative painting. Remained in Europe until 1946. Lives in Broomall, Pa.

89 *Synchromy To Form.* 1913-14. Oil, 11' 3" x 10' 3". Lent by the artist. *Ill. p. 50*

90 *Two Form: Synchromy No. 4.* 1914. Oil, 23½ x 20". Lent by the Pinacotheca Gallery, New York.

RUVOLO, FELIX

Born New York, 1912. Childhood spent in Sicily. Lived in Chicago, 1926-48. Studied at Art Institute of Chicago. First one-man show, Durand-Ruel Galleries, New York, 1947. Lives in Walnut Creek, California.

91 *Undulating Landscape.* 1950. Oil, 30 x 43¾". Lent by the Catherine Viviano Gallery, New York. *Ill. p. 115*

RYAN, ANNE

Born New Jersey, 1889. Studied Columbia University and with S. W. Hayter and Louis Shanker. First one-man show, New York, 1941. Lives in New York.

92 *No. 48.* 1950. Collage, 15¾ x 12½". The Museum of Modern Art, New York, Purchase Fund. *Ill. p. 115*

SCHAMBERG, MORTON L.

Born Philadelphia, 1881. Studied at University of Pennsylvania and at Pennsylvania Academy under William Chase. France, 1906-09, with Charles Sheeler; first in-

fluenced by Matisse and Cubism. About 1916 special interest in machine subjects. Exhibited in Armory Show, 1913, and with Society of Independent Artists, New York, 1917. Died 1918.

93 *Abstraction.* 1916. Oil, 39 x 20¼". Lent by the Louise and Walter Arensberg Collection, Hollywood. *Ill. p. 60*

94 *Machine.* 1916. Oil, 30⅛ x 22¾". Lent by the Yale University Art Gallery, New Haven, *Société Anonyme* Collection. *Ill. p. 61*

SELIGER, CHARLES

Born New York, 1926. Self-taught. First one-man show, Norlyst Gallery, New York, 1942. Lives in New York.

95 *Winterscape.* 1948-49. Tempera, 13⅝ x 11⅜". Lent by the Willard Gallery, New York. *Ill. p. 136*

SHAW, CHARLES G.

Born New York, 1892. Studied London, Paris, and Art Students League, New York. First one-man exhibition, Valentine Gallery, New York, 1934. Has exhibited with American Abstract Artists since 1937. Lives in New York.

95 *Force in Space.* 1950. Oil, 48 x 32". Lent by the Passedoit Gallery, New York. *Ill. p. 121*

SMITH, DAVID

Born Decatur, Indiana, 1906. Studied Ohio University, George Washington University and Art Students League. First one-man show, East River Gallery (Marian Willard), 1938. Workshop from 1934-41 in foundry on Brooklyn waterfront. Lives in Bolten Landing, N.Y.

97 *Amusement Park.* 1937. Steel with cadmium, 33¾" long. Lent by the Willard Gallery, New York. *Ill. p. 110*

98 *Blackburn: Song of an Irish Blacksmith.* 1949-1950. Iron, 46½" high. Lent by the Willard Gallery, New York. *Ill. p. 147*

SPENCER, NILES

Born Pawtucket, R.I., 1893. Studied Rhode Island School of Design, Art Students League and with Henri and Bellows. Influenced by Cubism, c. 1920-21. Europe: 1921-22 and 1928-29. First one-man show Daniel Gallery, New York, 1925. Renewed abstract emphasis in work from c. 1943. Lives in Dingmans Ferry, Pa.

99 *Two Bridges.* 1947. Oil, 28½ x 45½". Lent by Mr. and Mrs. Roy R. Neuberger, New York. *Ill. in color, p. 87*

STAMOS, THEODOROS

Born New York, 1922. Studied American Art School with Simon Kennedy. First one-man show, Wakefield Gallery, New York, 1943. Traveled in Europe 1943. Lives in New York.

100 *Sacrifice of Chronos, No. 2.* 1948. Oil, 48 x 36". Lent by The Phillips Gallery, Washington, D.C. *Ill. p. 140*

155

STELLA, JOSEPH

Born Muro-Lucano, Italy, 1877. Gave up medical studies for painting. To U.S. 1900. Studied New York School of Art, 1902. Italy, France, 1909-12. Exhibited Rome, 1910. Returned to U.S. 1912; style strongly influenced by Italian Futurism. Exhibited Armory Show, 1913; and with Society of Independent Artists, New York, 1917. Died New York, 1946.

101 *Spring.* 1914. Oil, 75 x 40⅛". Lent by the Yale University Art Gallery, New Haven, *Société Anonyme* Collection. *Ill. p. 42*

102 *Battle of Light, Coney Island.* 1914. Oil, 6' 3¾" x 7'. Lent by the Yale University Art Gallery, New Haven, *Société Anonyme* Collection. *Ill. p. 43*

103 *Brooklyn Bridge.* 1917-18. Oil, 7' x 6' 4". Lent by the Yale University Art Gallery, New Haven, *Société Anonyme* Collection. *Ill. p. 44*

TOBEY, MARK

Born Centerville, Wisconsin, 1890. Self-taught. First exhibited Knoedler, 1917. Traveled Europe and Near East, 1925-26. Lived in England, 1931-38. Traveled in Japan and China, 1934: studied Chinese calligraphy. Lives in Seattle.

104 *Tundra.* 1944. Tempera, 24 x 16½". Lent by the Willard Gallery, New York. *Color frontispiece*

TOMLIN, BRADLEY WALKER

Born Syracuse, N.Y., 1899. Studied Syracuse University. First one-man show Montross Gallery, New York, 1924. Began working in cubist direction c. 1934; turned to free calligraphic style, 1946. Lives in New York.

105 *No. 7.* 1950. Oil, 6' 8" x 3' 10". Lent by the Betty Parsons Gallery, New York. *Ill. p. 112*

WEBER, MAX

Born Bialystok, Russia, 1881. To U.S. 1891. Studied Pratt Institute under A. W. Dow, 1898-1901. To Europe 1905-08. Studied at several Paris academies; exhibited at Paris, *Salon des Indépendants* and *Salon d'Automne.* With P. H. Bruce and A. B. Frost, Jr. among first students of Henri Matisse, 1907-08. Returned to U.S. 1909; first one-man show at Haas Gallery, New York. Strong cubist and futurist influence, 1910-17. After 1918 returned to figurative painting. Lives in Great Neck, Long Island.

106 *New York.* 1912. Oil, 40 x 32". Lent by Wright Ludington, Santa Barbara. *Ill. p. 37*

107 *New York at Night.* 1915. Oil, 34½ x 22". Lent by A. P. Rosenberg & Co., Inc., New York. *Ill. p. 41*

108 *Rush Hour, New York.* 1915. Oil, 36¼ x 30¼". Lent by the artist. *Ill. p. 38*

BIBLIOGRAPHY

The following references, which, with one exception, are in the Museum Library, have been grouped into these sections: 1. American Titles: 1913-1950.—2. American Collections of Abstract Art.—3. Selected Exhibitions: 1913-1950. —4. General References.—5. Contemporary Sculpture. General bibliographies are noted in nos. 41, 45, 49, 60, 65, 76, 77. Unfortunately, lack of space makes it impossible to provide the convenience of a single author index, as well as citations for individual artists.

BERNARD KARPEL

I. AMERICAN TITLES: 1913—1950

1 GREGG, FREDERICK JAMES. For and against; views on the international exhibition held in New York and Chicago. 64 p. New York, Association of American painters and sculptors, inc., 1913.

2 LAURVIK, J. NILSEN. Is it art? Post-impressionism, futurism, cubism. 34 p. il. New York, International press, 1913.

3 DE ZAYAS, MARIUS & HAVILAND, PAUL B. A study of the modern evolution of plastic expression. 36 p. il. New York, "291," 1913.

4 PALMER, HARRIET, Compiler. [Armory Show scrapbook] 1913. *Unique collection of clippings, reviews, cartoons, etc. assembled from contemporary records. (Copy in Museum Library.)*

5 EDDY, ARTHUR JEROME. Cubists and post-impressionism. 273 p. 74 il. (pt.col.) Chicago, McClurg, 1914. *Written 1913; revision 1919. Bibliography.*

6 DANA, JOHN COTTON. American art, how it can be made to flourish. 31 p. Woodstock, Vt., Elm Tree press, 1914. *Second printing, 1929.*

7 WRIGHT, WILLARD HUNTINGTON. Modern painting, its tendency and meaning. 352 p. il. (pt. col.) New York & London, John Lane, 1915.

8 HARTLEY, MARSDEN. Adventures in the arts. 254 p. New York, Boni & Liveright, 1921.

9 CHENEY, SHELDON. A primer of modern art. 383 p. il. New York, Boni & Liveright, 1924. *Frequently reprinted.*

9a ROSENFELD, PAUL. Port of New York; essays on fourteen American moderns. 311 p. il. N. Y., Harcourt, Brace, 1924.

10 PACH, WALTER. Modern art in America. 69 p. incl. il. New York, C.W. Kraushaar galleries, 1928.

11 LaFOLLETTE, SUZANNE. Art in America. 361 p. il. New York & London, Harper, 1929.

12 KOOTZ, SAMUEL. Modern American painters. 64 p. plus 60 pl. New York, Brewer & Warren, 1930.

13 SAYLER, OLIVER. Revolt in the arts; a survey of the creation, distribution and appreciation of art in America. 351 p. New York, Brentano's, 1930.

14 ROTHSCHILD, EDWARD F. The meaning of unintelligibility in modern art. 103 p. Chicago, University of Chicago press, 1931.

15 RINGEL, FRED J., ed. America as Americans see it. 365 p. il. New York, Literary Guild, 1932.

16 KEPPEL, FREDERICK P. & DUFFUS, R. L. The arts in American life. 227 p. New York and London, McGraw-Hill book co., 1933.

17 AMERICA & ALFRED STIEGLITZ. A collective portrait; Waldo Frank, Lewis Mumford, Dorothy Norman, Paul Rosenfeld, and Harold Rugg, ed. 339 p. il. Garden City, N.Y., Doubleday, Doran, 1934.

18 CAHILL, HOLGER & BARR, ALFRED H., Jr. Art in America in modern times. 100 p. il. New York, Reynal & Hitchcock, 1934. Bibliography.

19 CHENEY, SHELDON. Expressionism in art. 415 p. il. New York, Liveright, 1934.

20 CRAVEN, THOMAS. Modern art: the men, the movements, the meaning. 377 p. il. New York, Simon and Schuster, 1934.

21 SWEENEY, JAMES JOHNSON. Plastic redirections in 20th century painting. 103 p. Chicago, University of Chicago press, 1934.

22 SOBY, JAMES THRALL. After Picasso. 114 p. il. Hartford, E. V. Mitchell; N.Y., Dodd, Mead, 1935.

23 ROURKE, CONSTANCE. Charles Sheeler, artist in the American tradition. il. New York, Harcourt, Brace, 1938.

24 GOLDWATER, ROBERT J. Primitivism in modern painting. 210 p. il. New York & London, Harper, 1938. Bibliographies, especially p. 207-8.

25 PACH, WALTER. Queer thing, painting; forty years in the world of art. 335 p. il. New York & London, Harper, 1938.

26 AMERICAN ABSTRACT ARTISTS. 30 p. plus 44 il. [New York, The Association, 1938].

27 ARMITAGE, MERLE. So called abstract art. 25 leaves, 1 col. pl. New York, E. Weyhe, 1939.

28 BOSWELL, PEYTON. Modern American painting. 230 p. incl. col. pl. New York, 1939.

29 CHENEY, MARTHA CANDLER. Modern art in America. 190 p. il. New York, London, Whittlesey house, 1939.

30 JEWELL, EDWARD ALLEN. Have we an American art? 232 p. il. New York & Toronto, Longmans, Green, 1939.

31 RICHARDSON, EDGAR PRESTON. The way of western art, 1776-1914. 204 p. il. Cambridge, Mass., Harvard university press, 1939.

32 SAINT-GAUDENS, HOMER. The American artist and his times. 332 p. il. New York, Dodd, Mead, 1941.

33 MELLQUIST, JEROME. The emergence of an American art. 421 p. il. New York, Scribner's, 1942.

34 PEARSON, RALPH M. Experiencing American pictures. p. 32-42, 170-224. New York, Harper, 1943.

35 JANIS, SIDNEY. Abstract and surrealist art in America. 146 p. il. (pt. col.) New York, Reynal & Hitchcock, 1944. Illustrations annotated by artist's statements.

36 KEPES, GYORGY. Language of vision; with introductory essays by S. Giedion and S. I. Hayakawa. 228 p. il. Chicago, Paul Theobald, 1944.

37 AMERICAN ABSTRACT ARTISTS. [68] p. incl. il. New York, Printed by the Ram press [for the Association], 1946. Distributed by Wittenborn, Schultz, New York.

38 HOFFMAN, FREDERICK J., ALLEN, CHARLES, ULRICH, CAROLYN F. The little magazine, a history and a bibliography. 440 p. Princeton, N.J., Princeton university press, 1946. Chronology of the avant-garde journal in America.

39 MOHOLY-NAGY, LÁSZLÓ. Vision in motion. 371 p. il. Chicago, Paul Theobald, 1947.

40 PUTNAM, SAMUEL. Paris was our mistress; memoirs of a lost and found generation. 264 p. New York, Viking press, 1947.

41 MONRO, ISABEL S. & MONRO, KATE M. Index to reproductions of American paintings; a guide to pictures occurring in more than eight hundred books. 731 p. New York, H. W. Wilson, 1948. List of books indexed, p. 11-26.

42 SOBY, JAMES THRALL. Contemporary painters. 151 p. il. New York, Museum of modern art, 1948.

43 BLANSHARD, FRANCES BRADSHAW. Retreat from likeness in the theory of painting. 2. ed. 178 p. il. New York, Columbia university press, 1949. Bibliography.

44 HAYTER, STANLEY WILLIAM. New ways of gravure. 274 p. il. New York, Pantheon books, 1949.

45 LARKIN, OLIVER W. Art and life in America. 574 p. il. New York, Rinehart, 1949. Extensive bibliographies. Pulitzer prize award.

46 LEEPA, ALLEN. The challenge of modern art. 256 p. il. New York, Beechhurst press, 1949.

47 RATHBUN, MARY CHALMERS & HAYES, BARTLETT H., Jr. Layman's guide to modern art; painting for a scientific age. n.p. il. New York, Oxford university press, 1949. Based on Addison gallery exhibition "Seeing the unseeable" (1947).

48 THREE LECTURES ON MODERN ART. [By K. S. Dreier, J. J. Sweeney, N. Gabo]. 91 p. il. New York, Philosophical library, 1949.

49 WIGHT, FREDERICK S. Milestones of American painting in our century. 135 p. il. Boston, Institute of contemporary art; New York, Chanticleer press, 1949. Bibliography.

50 COMMAGER, HENRY STEELE. The American mind, an interpretation of American thought and character since the 1880's. New Haven, Yale university press, 1950.

51 MYERS, BERNARD. Modern art in the making. 457 p. il. New York, Toronto, London, McGraw-Hill book co., 1950.

52 WEITZ, MORRIS. Philosophy of the arts. 239 p. Cambridge, Mass., Harvard university press, 1950.

53 MODERN ARTISTS IN AMERICA. Editors: Robert Motherwell, Ad Reinhardt. il. New York, Wittenborn,

Schultz, (in process). *"A study of the avant-garde in America" reviewing American painting and sculpture for the season 1949-50. Scheduled for spring 1951.*

II. AMERICAN COLLECTIONS OF ABSTRACT ART

54 NEW YORK UNIVERSITY. MUSEUM OF LIVING ART. Museum of living art, A. E. Gallatin collection. n.p. il. New York, 1940. *Opened 1927; other catalogs 1930, 1933, 1937; historical review Art News 42 no. 1:14-15, 27-8 Feb 15 1943.*

55 GUGGENHEIM, SOLOMON R. Art of tomorrow, fifth catalogue of the Solomon R. Guggenheim collection of non-objective paintings. 182 p. il. (pt. col.) New York, 1939. *Text by Hilla Rebay.*

56 ART OF THIS CENTURY, NEW YORK. Art of the century . . . 1910 to 1942. Edited by Peggy Guggenheim. 156 p. il. New York, 1942.

57 NEW YORK. MUSEUM OF MODERN ART. Painting and sculpture in the Museum of modern art. Edited by Alfred H. Barr, Jr. 327 p. il. N. Y., 1948. *Founded 1929; supplement Museum Bulletin 17 no. 2-3 1950.*

58 MILLER COMPANY, MERIDEN, CONN. Painting towards architecture. Text by Henry-Russell Hitchcock. 118 p. il. (pt. col.) N. Y., Duell, Sloan and Pearce, 1948.

59 CHICAGO. ART INSTITUTE. 20th century art from the Louise and Walter Arensberg collection. 104 p. il. 1949. *Pioneer collection exhibited Oct. 20-Dec. 18, 1949.*

60 NEW HAVEN, CONN. YALE UNIVERSITY ART GALLERY. Collection of the Société anonyme: Museum of modern art 1920. 223 p. il. New Haven, Conn., Associates in fine arts, Yale university, 1950. *List of exhibitions, lectures, publications (1920-1939). Katherine S. Dreier and Marcel Duchamp, Trustees. Extensive notes and bibliographies. Catalog ed. by G. H. Hamilton, curator.*

III. SELECTED EXHIBITIONS (1913-1950)

61 ASSOCIATION OF AMERICAN PAINTERS AND SCULPTORS, INC. Catalogue of international exhibition of modern art . . . at the Armory. 105 p. [New York, 1913]. *Exhibited Feb.-Mar.; variant catalogs for Boston and Chicago showings.*

62 THE FORUM, NEW YORK. The Forum exhibition of modern American painters. 14 p. il. New York, 1916. *Exhibited Mar. 13-25 at Anderson galleries.*

63 SOCIÉTÉ ANONYME (MUSEUM OF MODERN ART), NEW YORK. Catalogue of an international exhibition of modern art assembled by the Société anonyme, November 19, 1926 to January 1, 1927. [29] p. il. [Brooklyn, N. Y., Brooklyn museum, 1926]. *To be supplemented by Katherine S. Dreier: Modern Art. 117 p. il. New York, Société Anonyme, 1926.*

64 NEW YORK. WHITNEY MUSEUM OF AMERICAN ART. Abstract painting in America, February 12 to March 22. [20] p. il. New York, 1935. *Reviewed Magazine of Art 28: 168-70 Mar 1935.*

65 NEW YORK. MUSEUM OF MODERN ART. Cubism and abstract art, by Alfred H. Barr, Jr. 249 p. il. New York, 1936. *Bibliography.*

66 AMERICAN ABSTRACT ARTISTS. Exhibition, April 3-17, 1937 . . . Squibb galleries. 32 leaves in folder [New York, 1937]. *The AAA has issued yearbooks (1938, 1946) and annual checklists of exhibitions.*

67 ST. ETIENNE, GALERIE, NEW YORK. American abstract art, assembled by Stephan Lion. [4] p. 1940. *Exhibited May 22-June 12. Foreword by G. L. K. Morris.*

68 NEW ART CENTER, NEW YORK. Masters of abstract art. 42 p. il. New York, 1942. *Edited by Stephan C. Lion and Charmion Wiegand for Helena Rubinstein's gallery, Apr. 1-May 15. Texts by Davis, Holty, Morris, etc.*

69 SAN FRANCISCO. MUSEUM OF ART. Abstract and surrealist art in the United States. 36 p. il. San Francisco, 1944. *Circulating exhibition selected by Sidney Janis.*

70 NEW YORK. MUSEUM OF NON-OBJECTIVE ART. Loan exhibition April 15, 1944. *154 works, check list only. Another loan exhibition, Oct. 15, 1947.*

71 PHILADELPHIA. MUSEUM OF ART. Eight by eight, American abstract painting since 1940. [20] p. il. 1945. *Exhibited Mar. 7-Apr. 1. Preface by G. L. K. Morris.*

72 NEW YORK. WHITNEY MUSEUM OF AMERICAN ART. Pioneers of American art in America, April 9-May 19. 29 p. il. 1946. *Introduction by Lloyd Goodrich. Reviewed Art News 45:34-7, 65 Apr 1946.*

73 NEW YORK. MUSEUM OF MODERN ART. Fourteen Americans. Edited by Dorothy C. Miller, with statements by the artists and others. 80 p. il. New York, 1946. *Included Gorky, Motherwell, Noguchi, Pereira, Roszak, Tobey.*

74 CHICAGO. ART INSTITUTE. Abstract and surrealist American art. 63 p. il. Chicago, 1947. *58th American annual. "The first forty years" by K. Kuh (p. 6-18).*

75 URBANA, ILL. UNIVERSITY OF ILLINOIS. COLLEGE OF FINE AND APPLIED ARTS. Exhibition of contemporary American painting. 215 p. il. Urbana, Ill., 1950. *Exhibited Feb. 26-Apr. 2; extensive biographies.*

IV. GENERAL REFERENCES

76 MCCAUSLAND, ELIZABETH. A selected bibliography on American painting and sculpture from colonial times to the present. *Magazine of Art 39:329-49 Nov 1946.*

77 POHL, LA VERA ANN. Die Entwicklung der Malerei in Amerika von 1913-1938; inaugural-dissertation. 173 p. Bonn, Buchdruckerei J. F. Carthaus, 1939. *Thesis for Bonn University; chronological list of American museums and associations; index of foreign-born American artists; bibliography, p. 146-62.*

78 PHILADELPHIA. MUSEUM OF ART. History of an American, Alfred Stieglitz: "291" and after; selections from the Stieglitz collection. 48 p. il. 1944. *Reviewed by D. Grafly: The fathering of modern art in America. The Studio 130:148-50 Nov 1945. See also O. Larkin: Alfred Stieglitz and "291." Magazine of Art 40:178-83 May*

1947, and Fisk University. *Carl Van Vechten Gallery of Fine Arts. Catalogue of the Alfred Stieglitz collection for Fisk University. 48 p. il. 1949.*

79 FOUR MEMOIRS OF THE GROWTH OF ART AND TASTE IN AMERICA. il. *Art News* 37 no.22: 63-70, 153-6, 168-70, 172, 174, 178-9 Annual Number 1939. *Walt Kuhn, Henry McBride, D. G. Kelekian, S. A. Lewisohn.*

80 MELLQUIST, JEROME. The Armory show 30 years later. il. *Magazine of Art* 36:298-301 Dec 1943.

81 DASBURG, ANDREW. Cubism—its rise and influence. il. *The Arts* 4 no.5: 279-84 Nov 1923.

82 SCHACK, WILLIAM. On abstract painting; On abstract sculpture. il. *Magazine of Art* 27:470-5 Sept 1934; 27:580-8 Nov 1934. *Extended commentary by W. Abell: The limits of abstraction. 28:735-40 Dec 1935.*

83 SCHAPIRO, MEYER. Nature of abstract art. *Marxist Quarterly (New York)* 1 no.1:77-98 Jan-Mar 1937.

84 BALDINGER, W. S. Formal change in recent American painting, il. *Art Bulletin.* 19 no. 4: 580-91 Dec 1937.

85 PLASTIQUE. [American number] il. no.3 Printemps 1938. *Edited by S. H. Taeuber-Arp, A. E. Gallatin, G. L. K. Morris.*

86 DAVIS, STUART. Art & the masses. *Art Digest* 14 no.1:13, 34 Oct 1 1939. *On abstract art controversy recorded in the New York Times.*

87 AMERICAN ART AND THE MUSEUM. il. *Bulletin of the Museum of Modern Art (New York)* 7 no. 1 Nov 1940. *"A report of the extent and variety of what the Museum has done in the field of American art."*

88 DAVIS, STUART. Abstract art in the American scene. il. *Parnassus* 13:100-3 Mar 1941.

89 MORRIS, GEORGE L. K. On the mechanics of abstract painting. il. *Partisan Review* 8 no.5:403-17 Sept-Oct 1941.

90 LIFE OR DEATH FOR ABSTRACT ART? il. *Magazine of Art* 36:110-11, 117-9 Mar 1943. *Debate by Lincoln Kirstein and G. L. K. Morris.*

91 BROWN, MILTON W. Cubist-realism: an American style. il. *Marsyas (New York University)* 3:139-60 1943-45.

92 MOTHERWELL, ROBERT. Painter's objects. *Partisan Review* 11 no.1:93-7 Winter 1944.

93 PORTER, DAVID, GALLERY. Personal statement, painting prophecy, 1950. [16] p. Washington, D.C., David Porter, 1945. *Statements by American contemporaries for an exhibition held Feb 1945.*

94 GREENBERG, CLEMENT. The present prospects of American painting and sculpture. *Horizon* 16 no.93-4: 20-30 Oct 1947.

95 TYLER, PARKER. The humanism of abstract art. il. *Gazette des Beaux-Arts* 31:47-60 Jan-Feb 1947.

96 REINHARDT, ADOLPH F. How to look at modern art in America [a cartoon]. *Akron Art Institute* "Summer activities" number 1947 p.[7-8] 1947. *Cartoon from the New York paper P M.*

97 THE IDES OF ART: the attitudes of 10 artists on their art and contemporaneousness. il. *Tiger's Eye* (Westport, Conn.) no.2:42-6 Dec 1947.

98 POSSIBILITIES 1, Winter 1947/8. An occasional review [edited by Robert Motherwell and others] New York, Wittenborn, Schultz, 1948 (Problems of contemporary art.4) *Statements by Baziotes, Hayter, Motherwell, Pollock, Rothko, Smith.*

99 DEFENBACHER, D. S. Foreword. *In* Walker Art Center. Second biennial exhibition of paintings and prints. p. [6-7] Minneapolis, 1949.

100 SAN FRANCISCO ART ASSOCIATION. The western round table on modern art; abstract of proceedings. Edited by Douglas MacAgy. 71 p. (mimeographed) San Francisco, 1949.

101 A SYMPOSIUM: THE STATE OF AMERICAN ART. il. *Magazine of Art* 42:82-102 Mar 1949.

102 SUTTON, DENYS. The challenge of American art. *Horizon* 20 no.118:268-84 Oct 1949.

103 SEELEY, CAROL. On the nature of abstract painting in America. il. *Magazine of Art* 43:163-8 May 1950. *Previously published: Notes on the use of symbols in contemporary painting il.* Art Quarterly (Detroit) *no. 4:324-34 Autumn 1948.*

104 TANNENBAUM, LIBBY. Notes at mid-century. il. *Magazine of Art* 43 no.8:289-92 Dec 1950.

V. CONTEMPORARY SCULPTURE

105 GIEDION-WELCKER, CAROLA. Modern plastic art: elements of reality, volume and disintegration. 166 p. il. Zurich, H. Girsberger, 1937. (*Revision in process, 1951.*)

106 SEYMOUR, CHARLES. Tradition and experiment in modern sculpture. 86 p. il. Washington, D.C., American university press, 1949.

107 CUNLIFFE, MITZI SOLOMON. Earth and tools rediscovered. il. *Magazine of Art* 44:22-4 Jan 1951.

108 GREENBERG, CLEMENT. The new sculpture. *Partisan Review* 16:637-42 June 1949.

109 HOFMANN, HANS. Sculpture. *In his* Search for the real. p.55-9 Andover, Mass. Addison gallery of American art, 1948.

110 THE IDES OF ART: 14 SCULPTORS WRITE. il. *Tiger's Eye* (Westport, Conn.) no.4:73-107 June 1948.

111 CALDER, ALEXANDER. Mobiles. *In* Evans, Myfanwy, ed. The painter's object. p.62-7 il. London, Gerald Howe, 1937.

112 LIPPOLD, RICHARD. Variation number seven: Full moon. il. *Arts & Architecture* 67:22-3, 50 May 1950. *Additional commentary, 64:22-3 Aug 1947.*

113 LIPTON, SEYMOUR. Experience and sculptural form. *College Art Journal* 9 no.1:52-4 1949. *Additional "notes on my work."* Magazine of Art *40:264-5 Nov 1947.*

114 NOGUCHI, ISAMU. Meanings in modern sculpture. il. *Art News* 48:12-15, 55-6 Mar 1949. *Additional definitions,* Interiors *108:118-23 Mar 1949.*

115 ROSZAK, THEODORE J. Some problems of modern sculpture. il. *Magazine of Art* 42:53-6 Feb 1949.

116 SMITH, DAVID. Sculpture. il. *Architectural Record* 88 no.4:77-80 Oct 1940.

This book has been printed in January, 1951,
for the Trustees of the Museum of Modern Art, New York
by the Plantin Press, New York.

The color plates have been printed by
the John P. Smith Co., Rochester, New York.

Cover by Erik Nitsche